G000067576

# an Unjust hanging

## THE TRUE STORY OF JOHN HORWOOD

### SENT TO THE GALLOWS BY FOLLY, IGNORANCE AND A DOCTOR'S SELFISH CRUELTY

*Dave Halliwell*

## DAVE HALLIWELL

# an Unjust hanging

**MEMOIRS**

Cirencester

Published by Memoirs

MEMOIRS
PUBLISHING

25 Market Place, Cirencester, Gloucestershire, GL7 2NX
info@memoirsbooks.co.uk  www.memoirspublishing.com

Copyright ©Dave Halliwell July 2012

First published in England, July 2012

Book jacket design Ray Lipscombe

ISBN 978-1-909020-66-5

All rights reserved.

No part of this publication may be reproduced, stored in a retrieval system, or transmitted
in any form or by any means, electronic, mechanical, photocopying, recording or otherwise
without the prior permission of Memoirs.

Although the author and publisher have made every effort to ensure that the information in this
book was correct when going to press, we do not assume and hereby disclaim any liability to any
party for any loss, damage, or disruption caused by errors or omissions, whether such errors or
omissions result from negligence, accident, or any other cause. The views expressed in this book are
purely the author's.

Printed in England

# CONTENTS

Dedicated to Thomas and Phoebe Horwood and
Sarah Balsom of Hanham, who equally suffered the loss of a
loved one in tragic circumstances in 1821

# ACKNOWLEDGEMENTS

I would like to thank Mr Austin Williams & his fellow directors at E C Alderwick & Sons for their kindness & generosity in the laying to rest of John Horwood; Rev David Adams, for the sympathetic way in which he conducted the service; and numerous people, too many to mention individually, in the Bristol area and beyond who gave encouragement and support in bringing our quest to a satisfactory conclusion.

# INTRODUCTION

While researching the maternal side of my family, the Horwood/Harwoods of Nailsea in Somerset, I discovered from the 1851 Census that Thomas, my great-great-great grandfather, had been born in the parish of Bitton, Gloucestershire. I had no knowledge of Bitton, so I decided to search the internet, hoping to find out about its location, geography and history.

I stumbled upon a web page about the 'Book of Human Skin' held in Bristol Record Office, a collection of papers collected by Dr Richard Smith, who had dissected the body of John Horwood in 1821 at Bristol after he had been convicted of the murder of his ex-girlfriend by throwing a stone at her after she had refused his advances. The same web page claimed his skeleton was in the Bristol University Medical School and was still used for teaching purposes.

I discovered that the murder had taken place in Hanham in the parish of Bitton, the birthplace of my ancestor. I began to wonder if John Horwood the murderer was also one of my ancestors.

I contacted the Bristol & Avon Family History Society to seek advice, and the resulting information proved invaluable. Baptism records of Bitton proved that Thomas and John were brothers, two of ten children born to Thomas and Phoebe Horwood of Hanham.

After discovering this tragic and shocking family story, my curiosity was aroused and I decided to visit the Bristol area. Accompanied by my cousin Marie, I left my home in Lancashire in July 2009 with pre-arranged appointments to view both the skeleton and the book which had apparently been bound in our ancestor's skin.

On the day of arrival our first encounter with the past was a visit to the prison on Cumberland Road, Bristol, the place of John Horwood's execution. The building has been demolished and only the main gate remains, but we found it very moving and upsetting being at the place where our ancestor's life had so brutally ended.

The next day we had an appointment with Angela Wells at the Bristol University Medical School to view John's skeleton. After satisfying security we were allowed into the building, where Angela was waiting for us. After the introductions we followed her up two flights of stairs before she stopped by the side of the next stairwell. Here she opened a padlocked cupboard door, revealing a wooden case rather like the case of a grandfather clock, with a glass door front.

Suspended inside by a brass hook attached to the top of the skull was the skeleton of John Horwood, still with a rope around his neck.

Before I could say anything, Angela explained that the rope was there to show that the skeleton was that of a felon, and began to explain why it was kept where it was. It seemed that after a broadcast on the subject a number of years earlier by BBC Bristol they had been inundated with requests from the general public to view the skeleton. The legal department had decided to remove it from public view in case a family member objected. Angela informed us that we were the first family members to approach them.

She then took another key and unlocked the door of the case, opening it wide. It was then that I noticed that the skeleton had very large hands; my grandfather also had very large hands. I placed my hand on the shoulder of the skeleton and closed my eyes, silently saying 'God bless you'.

Marie and I were then informed that the skeleton belonged to us and we could do with it whatever we wished. This was a complete shock to both of us, and we stared at each other in amazement. The visit left us with a deep sorrow in our hearts and a great deal to discuss as to what we could do with the skeleton.

Later the same day we visited Hanham, where our first call was to the beautiful church of St George in Hanham Abbotts. Unfortunately the church was locked. I was a little disappointed that we could not gain entry, but still enjoyed the visit.

Christ Church was our next call, and here, luckily, the verger was in attendance. He was very helpful in our search for the grave of Thomas Horwood, my four-greats grandfather and the father of the unfortunate John, who had been buried in the churchyard in 1845. Unfortunately no headstone could be found.

The following morning we had an appointment at Bristol Records Office to view the book which had been bound in John Horwood's skin. After going through the usual security checks we were introduced to Katie Petty, who escorted us into a research room. She wore white gloves and explained that we must not touch the book, owing to its fragile condition. She removed the book from a box and gently placed it on to a white cushion, taking great care when handling it.

The first thing I noticed was the awful smell - I can only describe it as rotting leather. With age it had turned dark brown, but I could see the skull and crossbones embossed in each corner and the inscription 'Cutis Vera Johannis Horwood' translated as 'The Skin of John Horwood'.

My visit to Bristol over, I returned home to Lancashire determined to find out how Eliza and John had met their tragic deaths. What I was to discover would shock me and my family to the core.


**Mary Halliwell**

John Horwood

# CHAPTER ONE

## *Born into poverty*

The hamlet of Hanham in the parish of Bitton lies four and a half miles from Bristol on the main A4 Bath road and covers an area of 1195 acres, much of it used for agriculture. The hamlet lies in an area known as Kingswood, at one time one of the hunting grounds of the Kings of England. The forest now long gone, the inhabitants occupy themselves in the manufacture of pins, brass, spelter, zinc, iron, chemicals, hats, felt, boots, shoes, soap, candles, the quarrying of Pennant stone and the mining of coal.

The coalpits here employed a vast number of the residents, and the loss of life was so bad that deaths were expected almost on a daily basis. Children were not exempt from this dangerous occupation, family members employing them to drag the full coal tubs from the coal face to the shaft and the empty ones back, keeping the wages in the household through necessity. Some of those boys and girls were of such a tender age that fathers would carry them on their backs to the pit, where the timid ones were placed in a sack until they reached the working place underground. At this time there were no regulations imposed on the owners. It was not until the Coal Mines Act of 1842 that children under the age of ten and women were stopped from working underground.

The miners of Kingswood were a hardy lot who feared no one,

and on many occasions they confronted the authorities with force and rioted to protect their employment interests against interference from outsiders. They had nothing else and many knew nothing else; their work in the coal pits was their only salvation.

The manufacture of brass, spelter (zinc alloy), iron and chemicals would have been carried out in works built for these purposes, whereas pins, hats, felt, boots, shoes, soaps and candles would have been partly or wholly manufactured in the factory or in the workers' homes. They were paid so much for completing so many items. Wages were kept low by a surplus of labour; numbers needed in the agricultural industry were declining because of the invention of new machinery.

The majority of the inhabitants were good, hard-working people. Although poor, they were law-abiding and expected very little out of life. There was however a minority who found life was made easier by stealing from others rather than working for their daily bread, and Hanham was described as the most unruly place in the kingdom. This was a reference to the Cockroad gang, who had for more than fifty years past lived on the proceeds of their crimes. Certain families had for three or more generations terrorized the district with highway robbery and burglary and demands for protection money.

The haunt of the gang was the Blue Bowl Inn, an ancient establishment claimed to be one of the oldest inns in the country and said by some to date back to Roman times. This inn stands on the Cock Road, the main route between Bristol and Bath, which was used by merchants doing business in both cities. The gang frequently relieved them of their money in Hanham. Over the years many highwaymen were caught and hanged, but this did not deter the others and there was always another thief to take the place of the man who had swung from the gibbet.

The Cockroad Gang had so many members that more than one property would be robbed at the same time. Travellers were stopped on the highway in daylight or darkness alike, grossly insulted and robbed. Gangs of ruffians were always on the lookout at vantage points on the road, giving them time to prepare for the robbery. Cock Road was a den of universal terror. The gang members sallied forth to commit their crimes in Bristol, Bath, Gloucester and further afield, returning with their plunder. Farmers would arrive in Hanham accompanied by constables in search of missing livestock, and the gang would take great pleasure in showing them their own pigs or sheep, butchered and dressed into cuts of meat, which of course they could not identify as theirs.

In 1815 the Bristol authorities decided to take drastic action against the gang. They knew their names and where they lived. The Bristol watchmen were assembled, and in the still of the night they proceeded to the thieves' stronghold. They quietly surrounded their houses and took all the male occupants into custody. Twenty-five prisoners were thrown into Gloucester Jail, charged with various offences.

These arrests put an end at last to the antics of the Cockroad Gang. Those in custody stood trial. Some were hanged and others transported to Australia for the rest of their lives.

It was 1813 before the first school was opened in Hanham, by the Wesleyans. Seventy-five children turned up on the first day, and of these only seventeen knew even part of the alphabet and none could read. It was said at the time that all these children were entirely dependent on a culture of robbery and plunder for their support.

Religion was not part of the majority of inhabitants' lives, although it is well documented that an improvement was noticed with the coming of the Methodist Church Ministry into these parts. In reality this world had nothing to offer them except hopes of a better life in the next, as long as they led good, clean and honest lives.

Thomas Horwood was born in Hanham in 1762, and at the age of twelve he went to sea. His last voyage was to the East Indies, from which he returned to Hanham in 1786. Before returning home he spent some time in London, where he met and courted his future wife, Phoebe Palantine. Phoebe had left her birthplace in Orkney to seek a position in London and was employed as a servant when she met Thomas.

The courtship flourished and Thomas brought Phoebe from London to Hanham, where they married in 1786. The couple were highly respected by all who knew them. Together they had ten children, four girls and six boys. Two of the girls, and the last born, William, died in infancy. Among the surviving siblings were twin sons, James and Joseph, the former born in the last minutes of a Monday, the latter very early on a Tuesday.

When they became old enough, they and their elder brother Thomas went to work in the coal pits. In 1806, at the age of fifteen, Joseph was brought home from work in the colliery cart with a broken leg, having had a very narrow escape from death while at work in the pit. Just ten days later, the same cart was at the door again; this time it was James lying on his back in the cart covered by a sack, and he had not been so lucky. He had been killed at the Pile Marsh Pit about three hours after leaving for work. His death was caused by the breaking of the rope securing the suspension of the cage, causing it to fall 20 fathoms (120 feet) to the bottom of the shaft as he and four others were descending. Four men in all lost their lives, while the fifth was gravely injured.

The death of his twin brother had a great effect on Joseph.

When he had sufficiently recovered from his broken leg, he reluctantly returned to the pit, where he worked in great terror. As soon as he could he obtained work in the stone quarry, and laboured there ever after.

Oldest brother Thomas had married in 1815 and set up home in Nailsea, Somerset, after securing employment at the Nailsea Glass Works. Joseph had married and lived in Hanham. Samuel left in 1815 to seek work in the North of England, marrying a local girl up in Northumberland. The oldest girl, Catherine, had married and lived next door to her parents. The youngest, Mary, still lived at home with her parents and younger brother, John.

John Horwood began his working life as a young boy in the coal pits, as his elder brothers had done. He had worked in the pits for about two years when a series of accidents occurred within a short time, one after another. He became very concerned for his own safety and refused to continue in the pit.

Eliza Balsom was born nearby in the same year as John Horwood, 1803. They knew each other from infancy, both the poor, uneducated children of hard-working but honest families surrounded by a world of crime. Eliza was the daughter of Sarah Balsom. Sarah's husband Richard had died, leaving the widowed mother to bring up her family alone.

John fell for Eliza, but it seems she did not want him quite as much as he wanted her. Her rejection of him was to bring them both to tragic ends.

# CHAPTER TWO

*A tragic encounter*

The records show that on 31st January 1821, Dr Richard Smith at Bristol Royal Infirmary treated Eliza for a head wound. At first the wound was not considered too serious, but alarming symptoms began to develop, so he reported the circumstances of the injury to the magistrates, Mr Day and Alderman Haythorne. Day and Haythorne went to the Infirmary and took a statement from the injured girl. She told them that John Horwood had thrown a stone with the intention of killing her. A warrant was issued for Horwood's arrest on a charge of assault.

The magistrates instructed two Yeoman Sheriffs, messrs Bull and Sew, to proceed to Hanham early the following morning, 15th February, to arrest John Horwood. The two men left Bristol by private carriage and called at the home of Eliza's mother to ask directions to Horwood's cottage. When they got there they found his aged mother poorly in bed, being looked after by her married daughter. Horwood's father had left for work.

Horwood's sister Catherine lived next door. Horwood's door was not locked and they burst in, asking where John was. She demanded to know why they wanted him and asked to see the warrant for his arrest, blocking their way to the stairs. At this one of the men drew a pistol and placed it behind her ear, and she was manhandled out of the way.

Horwood heard them arrive and guessed their errand. Still in his nightshirt, he attempted escape through the bedroom window. Finding it too narrow, he picked up a quarryman's hammer and stood his ground at the top of the stairs, threatening the destruction of all who dared approach him.

He swung blow after blow in the direction of Bull and Sew. At one point it was thought their pistols would have to be fired to bring him down. Horwood aimed a great many blows at them with the hammer, but they managed to parry them with their bludgeons.

After putting up much resistance, Horwood eventually began to tire. In one last attempt at escape he threw the hammer with all his might at Bull, striking him a glancing blow above his eye. Fortunately this caused little damage.

The officers managed to close in on him and knock him down. After a desperate struggle they handcuffed him and dragged him into the carriage, which sped away with haste in the direction of Bristol.

The carriage pulled up outside the Bristol Infirmary and Horwood was taken to the consulting room to wait until the magistrates arrived. He seemed indifferent and displayed a vulgar, couldn't-care-less attitude to those who had arrested him. Dr Richard Smith decided to teach him a lesson and shock him to arouse his senses. He unlocked a cupboard kept in that room which contained the skeletons of Maria Davies and Charlotte Bobbitt, who had been hanged on St Michaels Hill in 1802 for murdering a child. He told Horwood who the skeletons belonged to. Although this made him a little quieter, Horwood still seemed indifferent.

Horwood was taken to Eliza's bedside with Dr Smith and the two magistrates in attendance. Smith said to Eliza, 'Here is Horwood close by, would you be afraid to see him?' She replied, 'Yes, he will kill me.' Smith said 'I will prevent that. Alderman

Haythorne wishes to speak with you, do not be afraid of anything.'

Eliza then pulled herself up and began to look around. Smith pointed to Horwood and said, 'Do you know that man?' She replied, 'Yes, that is the villain that murdered me.' Horwood muttered, 'I...' and Eliza interrupted, saying, 'He threw a stone at me.' Smith asked her to look at him again and confirm that he was the person who had thrown the stone. She replied, 'No, I am afraid, I do not wish to see the villain.'

As she turned away, the Alderman asked Horwood 'Would you like me to ask her any questions?' 'No, but I did not do it' he said. He then turned to Dr Smith, who was standing beside him, saying, 'I know who did it, but it wasn't me.' Horwood was remanded in custody to Bridewell Police Station.

Eliza was by now very poorly, as the seemingly minor injury caused by the stone had become infected. Her mother treated the wound with ointment, a bread poultice and bandage.

At first Eliza went about the house and even did some work. On the 30th January she walked to the infirmary for treatment as an out-patient and on the morning of the 31st January, while she was waiting her turn for treatment, Dr Smith saw her with a bandage on her head. After inquiring what was wrong with her, he insisted that he should deal with her.

After examining Eliza he advised her to be admitted to the infirmary, as from his experience he knew how dangerous even slight injuries to the head could be. She was very reluctant to be admitted to the ward, but was eventually persuaded.

By the 10th February the wound had become inflamed and Eliza had become feverish. She was restless and suffered a very bad headache. Smith consulted with his five brethren in office and on the same day the seat of the injury was trephined (a hole drilled into her skull) by him. A small quantity of matter was found between the *dura* mater and bone. At first this gave Eliza some relief, but a relapse occurred and seven days later she died, of arachnoiditis (inflammation of the membrane around the brain) and a cerebral abscess. She was 18 years old.

An inquest into the circumstances of the girl's death was held on the Monday at the Full Moon Inn, North Street, Stokes Croft, Bristol. The Coroner, Joseph Langley Esq, presided. The whole affair took three hours and the Coroner's jury, after considering the evidence, returned a verdict of wilful murder by John Horwood. He was remanded to Bristol Gaol for trial at the next Assizes on a charge of the murder of Eliza Balsom.

After the inquest Eliza's body was released to her mother for burial. The funeral was held on Sunday 25th February 1821 and she was interred in St Mary's Churchyard in Bitton, probably in the same grave as her father.

After giving up mining and being out of work for a while, John had got a position at the local spelter works, which belonged to Philip George. John's father Thomas had been employed there for many years. John had seemed  a lot more at ease in this employment than in the pits, but about eighteen months before Eliza's death, due to lack of orders, Mr George had found it necessary to cut back on his labour at the works. Several men were dismissed, and unfortunately John was among them.

Very soon after losing his job he began to associate with idle and loose characters from the district. It was at this time he began to mix with Eliza and her friends. He was spending more and more time idling with his friends and less time looking for work. On occasions he conned his parents into buying him clothes on the pretence of looking for work, when all the time he wanted the clothes to try to impress Eliza.

During the fruit season he would pilfer, even in broad daylight and in full view of anyone passing at the time. He would raid the orchard of an old man any time he felt like it, in the man's full view, then run away laughing at him. What was stolen was usually sold to buy tobacco. On one occasion, he and Eliza's brother were caught in an orchard with stolen fruit and apprehended by the neighbours. For that he and the brother served one week in prison.

Young Horwood was suspected of much more serious crimes than stealing fruit, but no evidence could be brought against him. His father was becoming increasingly concerned about his behaviour, telling him to spend his time seeking employment instead of idling about with his friends. Thomas told him that he and his mother could not and would not afford to keep him.

His mother was always tender and loving towards him and would frequently feed him from the cupboard when his father was out of the house. For the past fourteen years she had been a member of the local Methodist Society, but she had never been able to persuade John to attend the chapel.

Eliza and John had become close to each other, courting during the summer months of 1820 and spending more and more time in each other's company. Towards the end of that year, according to local gossip, he was putting proposals to her, which she rejected. His proposals turned to threats and she became alarmed at his behaviour. She claimed his conduct became so bad that she was doing her best to avoid him.

On one occasion he assaulted her and she had to put herself under the protection of some nearby men. On another occasion he threw oil of vitriol over her, destroying her clothes (oil of vitriol, better known as sulphuric acid, can cause severe burns and eye damage). Then he waylaid her in a lane with what she thought was the intention to murder her, but she screamed and ran as fast as she could, reaching the safety of her home before he could catch up with her. After this she became afraid to go out, telling her mother that if she did, Horwood would 'surely be the death of her'.

On the 22nd of January 1821, Eliza's mother asked her to deliver some fruit to Bristol. On her way back that night, well after dark, she was spotted by Horwood, who was with two brothers, Joseph and William Fry, and a fourth youth, Thomas Barnes. Eliza was with Joseph Reece and William Waddy. Waddy was her new boyfriend, since Horwood had gone out of favour.

Horwood was on a hillside about forty yards from Eliza. As she began to cross the stream, he stooped down and scooped up a stone, then with all his might he threw it at her, striking her on the right side of her head.

She was stunned by the blow and stumbled into the stream, pulling William Waddy with her. It is claimed that one of Horwood's companions said, 'There, you've done it at last'. Then the trio ran off. Eliza was carried home by her friends.

On hearing that John had been charged with murder and was banged up in prison awaiting trial, the other Horwood sons sent money to their father to help with the hiring of a solicitor to defend him. A letter from Samuel Horwood and his wife follows:

Langley Mills, Northumberland, February 28th, 1821.

**Dear Father and Mother**

*We write these few lines to let you know we are well at present, thank God for it. But your letter, this day, has put us in the greatest trouble; I fear we shall have occasion never to forget. My trouble is so great about my dear brother, that it is not in my power to express it. I thought I would*

*die when I read the letter. I can be at no rest thinking on him. My dreams have been so bad, that I expected to hear bad news. My trouble increases when I think of my mother and think of her grief. I should have been thankful to Almighty God if it had been his will to have taken him before this unhappy trial. It shall be my constant prayers that he will take him to rest. Harvey says, in his Meditations, speaking of the grief's of a parent, 'Farewell, Farewell, my Son, my Son, I would to God I died for thee; Farewell my Child and Farewell all my earthly happiness; I shall never, never forget thee; never more see good in the land of the living. Attempt not to comfort me. I will go on mourning all my days, till my grey hairs go down with sorrow to the grave.' Love to all my Brothers and Sisters; but with grief. You must go into Bristol and see Counsel; and lay your case before him and see what he will plead for. Send me up word what the Counsel will plead for and send me a letter soon as possible and I will send you all the money I can get. No more at present from your troubled Son and Daughter.*
*Samuel and Ann Horwood.*

After help with the fees had been promised by family members, Thomas Horwood appointed solicitors Smith and Broderipp to defend his son.

# CHAPTER THREE

## *Murder charge*

John Horwood had initially been arrested on a charge of assault and held in custody at Bridewell in Bristol. After the death of Eliza and the subsequent coroner's inquest on the 19th February, the charge became one of wilful murder. On this more serious offence he was transferred from Bridewell to the New Prison at Bristol.

Bristol New Prison was commissioned in 1816 for a budget of £60,000, paid for by the ratepayers of the City. It opened its doors in 1820, and among the first inmates were prisoners transferred from Bristol's infamous Newgate Prison, which it replaced. This description is from Matthew's Bristol, Clifton and Hotwells Guide, published in 1825: 'This is an extensive and commodious building, for health, convenience and excellent arrangement is not to be equalled in England, commanding extensive views of the surrounding countryside. The boundary wall twenty feet high is hewn of variegated marble which has a beautiful appearance.'

The prison was built to hold 197 prisoners of mixed sex, and was a great improvement over its predecessors; Bridewell's prisoners had to have a cat put into their cells at night to stop rats from gnawing their feet. The new accommodation consisted of single cells, each measuring six feet by nine. Male and female prisoners were kept strictly apart, each having separate sections within its walls. Water supplies were drawn from a well using a large treadmill, and twenty prisoners at a time took their turn in bringing the water up. Prisoners were allowed a bath once a week, and the water needed for bathing alone would keep the prisoners busy on the treadmill. Inside the prison small windows restricted the flow of air circulating, which created a stale and fetid interior. Prisoners were poorly clothed and suffered from cold, especially in the winter months. At night the whole of the prison was enveloped in a shroud of darkness which even hampered the turnkeys in carrying out their duties.

The deposition Eliza had given to the magistrates on her death-bed alleged that John Horwood had frequently made indelicate and improper proposals to her. She had constantly refused to yield to his solicitations, and in consequence Horwood had several times threatened to murder her. The previous Christmas he had flung a quantity of oil of vitriol, or some other liquid, burning her clothes. He had waylaid her with intent, she believed, to kill her. Towards the end of January while walking in a lane at Hanham, he had got within a yard of her, and she had run home and alerted her family, who had come out, when he ran away. The following evening at eight or nine o'clock she had seen Horwood a short distance from her. He had sworn at her and said he would kill her, then taken up a stone, thrown it and struck her on the head, causing her to fall down. She had recollected nothing after that.

John Horwood was arrested on the 15th February and taken to Eliza's bedside at the infirmary. Her deposition was read to him in her presence. The magistrates gave him the chance to question her on it, but he declined.

Later that day the magistrates again questioned him on her allegations:

"Did you throw the stone at Eliza?"

"No, I am innocent of flinging the stone. I was present when some other person flung it at her. Samuel Fry, William Fry and Thomas Barnes were with me at the time."

"How long have you known Eliza?"

"As long as I have known myself."

"Did you throw vitriol over her?"

"I have never flung vitriol over her."

"Did you ever threaten her life?"

"I have never threatened her life."

It was noted by the magistrate that Horwood was uneducated and could neither read or write. He admitted that when courting and playing together Eliza had played with his ears and he had said in fun, 'If thee don't let alone my ears I'll kill thee.'

Eliza claimed he had thrown the vitriol over her at some time over Christmas, burning her clothes and ruining them. The prisoner denied this and claimed Eliza had told many lies against him. The prisoner's father had made enquiries into the claim and discovered that the dress Eliza wore belonged to her sister and the only damage was a very small hole and a couple of stains.

The defence had witness statements that the couple were still on the best of terms at a dance at the Ship public house on Boxing Day, the day the vitriol attack was supposed to have happened.

Mrs Jones was an old lady who had a small two-roomed cottage, one room up and one down. She would testify that on the night of New Year's Day Eliza and John had been together in her cottage until seven in the morning; she had left them by the hearth when she retired to her bed. John had shared his coat with Eliza because she was cold. Mrs Jones confirmed that they were on the best of terms at the New Year and very affectionate towards each other, loving her too much to hurt her. The evidence of this witness was not heard by the jury as Mrs Jones was ill on the day of the trial.

Locals stated that the place where the stone-throwing incident took place was the playground of the young children and the haunt of the older ones. The stream running through the valley attracted them and gave them an abundance of stones, which they would throw at targets from an early age. As they got older the children became so good that they could hit a target from forty or fifty yards with ease, hardly missing their aim in one out of ten throws, at times throwing at each other.

It was reported that John ran away from the scene after Eliza was struck. He claimed that he and Samuel Fry walked to the gate of Eliza's brother's house, asking some boys gathered there what the matter was. They had told him that Eliza had been struck by a stone, but no one knew who had thrown it. He also claimed that a few moments after he arrived some other young men had appeared at the house from the direction of the opposite bank of the brook, saying that one of them could have thrown the stone. He claimed that Eliza was walking away from where Horwood was standing, and unless she had turned her head round it would have been impossible to hit her over her right eye from that direction.

Ann Fry, a witness for the prosecution, said she had been at Eliza's brother's house when Eliza had arrived with her head cut. She had suggested a poultice of salt butter and brown paper. Eliza's brother cut her hair with scissors and shaved her scalp round the wound with his razor before applying the remedy suggested by her. Ann claimed she had heard Horwood make threats against Eliza and had also seen him with a bottle containing oil of vitriol, which he had thrown over her as well as Eliza.

The defence commissioned a detailed map of the scene, showing exactly the position of the prisoner and those with him and Eliza and her companions, as described by the witnesses. They were hoping to prove that from where Horwood had been he could neither have seen her or hit her with a stone over her eye, because she had had her back to him.

Interviewed by the defense, Waddy claimed that he and Eliza, when courting, had swapped partners with another couple they were friendly with, but he emphasized nothing improper had taken place. Dr Richard Smith had revealed at the inquest into Eliza's death that she was a virgin.

Mary Bull recalled a conversation she had heard between two of the chief prosecution witnesses, Barnes and Brooks. One of them had said 'Keep this up and we will have twenty pounds apiece to feast away with.' If true, it would indicate that they were being bribed by someone in exchange for giving evidence to guarantee a guilty verdict.

Samuel Wilmot, alias Brooks, was a prosecution witness who claimed to have heard Horwood make threats against Eliza's life. He had begun to use the name Brooks after his elder brother had been transported to the New World for his crimes a few years previously. Wilmot had declared to Horwood's mother that he knew nothing. Eliza's brother afterwards had called on him and had said that if someone else had not done for her, he would.

Thomas Barnes had informed Eliza's mother that he had seen John Horwood throw the stone, and had given this evidence at the inquest. This was before Eliza was taken to the infirmary. He was a sailor in the navy who had come home to Hanham on leave from his ship. He came home with money in his pocket and spent most of his time drinking in various public houses round about, but his local was the Ship at Hanham.

Eliza was very poorly in the infirmary and before John Horwood was arrested there had been bad blood between him and Barnes. Horwood had confronted him and asked him if it was true what he had heard, 'that it was thee who said I threw the stone.' Barnes had replied, 'would you like to know?' and again Horwood had asked him and Barnes had given the same reply. Horwood had asked, 'Do you wish to take my life, just tell me one way or the other.'

Horwood had then offered to fight Barnes, but he had declined, unless it was for money (he knew John had no money). Horwood had told him he would fight him for a bellyfull (of beer) and at this point had begun to take off his clothes, preparing for the fight. Barnes, not wanting a beating, threatened him, 'I'll do you over the girl.'

When Eliza died and Barnes went to Bristol to give evidence at the inquest, he arrived early and spent his time in a public house, so by the time he was called, he was drunk. The next day he could not remember a word of the evidence he had given. He had been drinking in the Ship before he met Horwood on the night of the incident. The defence should have had no trouble in discrediting the evidence of this witness, but William Fry had stated at the inquest that John's arm was up as if he had thrown something - this was not good for the defence.

In February the *Bristol Mercury*, under the headline 'SHOCKING OUTRAGE', published a full account of what it believed was the story, using sensational terms such as 'UNFEELING DEPRAVITY'. The newspaper quoted neighbours in Hanham as their source. This paper would have been read by those selected to serve on the jury, and it was feared it could influence the outcome.

A newspaper reported that some of Horwood's friends who had given evidence at the inquest had climbed up trees on Rope Walk, close to the prison. They had managed to communicate with their confined friend and assured him they would say nothing at his trial that would do him harm.

It had been reported that John Horwood was 28 years old, and the defence were concerned that the fact that he was ten years older than Eliza could have an effect on the minds of the jury at the trial. They requested a copy of his entry of baptism from the register at the church of St George that confirmed he was not yet 18 years old.

Before the trial began, a Grand Jury assembled to determine whether there was enough evidence for the charge to be heard in the Crown Court. The law at this time was that a Grand Jury had to meet to assess the indictments against the accused. Witnesses for the prosecution could testify before this jury, but not the witnesses of the defendant. In this case it seems there was a doubt if the charge should be murder or manslaughter, as he was charged with murder on the Coroner's Jury warrant.

In this case twenty-four jurymen scrutinized the evidence and out of these, four thought the charge should be changed from one of murder to manslaughter, while the other twenty thought murder to be the correct charge. Stephen Cave acted as Jury Foreman.

There was some confusion as to when the murder actually took place. Prosecution said it was 22nd January, while the defence said 14th or 21st January. Witness dates do not agree. Thomas Barnes said it was on or about the 21st, Eliza's mother and her next door neighbour Samuel Rogers claimed the 22nd, William Fry and William Waddy said 1st February and Joseph Reece said it was 8th February. The indictment against John Horwood gave the date as

22nd January, which was a Monday. Eliza had sought treatment at the Infirmary on Tuesday 30th and admitted on Wednesday 31st, over a week after the wounding.

John Horwood was accommodated in a solitary cell measuring six feet by nine and would have mixed with the other prisoners at mealtimes and while exercising. Everyone told him that there was no way he would hang for throwing a stone, and this reflected in his belief that he would be a free man after the trial. It seems he did not fully understand the perilous situation he was in. He had been found responsible for Eliza's death by the Coroner's Jury, resulting in him facing a charge of murder, and twenty out of twenty-four jurymen at the pre-trial investigation considered he should stand trial for murder rather than manslaughter. If he was found guilty by the Grand Jury at the Assizes, he would face execution.

The law as it stood at the time was an Act of Parliament passed in 1752, which became a Statute in British Law after Easter in that year, declaring that the bodies of felons executed for murder were to be handed over to surgeons for dissection.

While in prison Horwood was visited many times by the Reverend Roberts. He received him very respectfully and paid attention to what he said, but as he was expecting to be found not guilty, the Reverend made very little religious impression on him. All he got was promises to mend his ways when he got out, an undertaking which was very much doubted. The Reverend Roberts noted his youthful appearance. He was not yet eighteen, his young mind was muddled with ignorance and he could neither read nor write. He was all the more confident that he would be acquitted since hearing that the principle witness, Thomas Barnes, had gone to sea, but the Reverend informed him that he had been brought back under a Judge's Warrant and therefore would give evidence

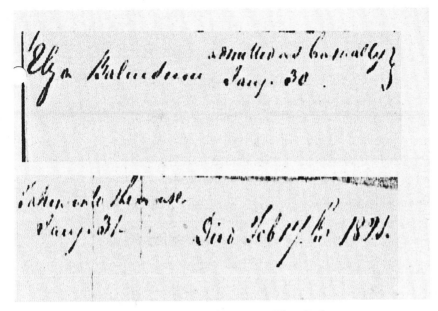

Infirmary records referring to Eliza Balsom

John Horwood standing at the bar during his trial

# DEATH OF E. BALSAM.

## A PARTICULAR ACCOUNT OF

the Apprehension and Commitment to Bridewell yesterday (Thursday, February 15, 1821) previous
to his being sent to Gloucester Goal,—of

# JOHN HORWOOD.

Of Kingswood, St. George's, near Bristol; for attempting, through Jealousy, to

# MURDER ELIZABETH BALSAM,

Of the same place, (his Sweetheart) by nearly beating her brains out with a stone, so that she lies
at our Infirmary without hopes of recovery.

From the information we have received of this diabolical affair, we have been able to gather the
following interesting particulars :—

John Horwood had for some time kept company with the unfortunate Elizabeth Balsam, but
for no other intention than to gratify his own lustful appetite, and at length he made a proposal to
her for that purpose; but she resented his base attack upon her virtue and declared she would drop
his company if he did not desist from such unwarrantable proceedings.

Horwood, however, persevered in his wicked intention, and contrived to inveigle the poor girl
one night to a lonely field, where he tried to accomplish his views; but she made a most resistance,
got from his grasp, and ran home as fast as she could; he threatening her life with most horrid im-
precations, and said, whenever he met her again he would certainly murder her.

On a day se'nnight, as she was going to the well for some water, he way-laid her, and once
more insulted her, but she made an equal resistance as before, upon which he took up a large stone,
and with the utmost savage ferocity nearly beat her skull to pieces. Her screams, however, brought
her friends to her assistance; but she was so seriously injured, that it was found advisable to send her
to our Infirmary, where she now lies at the point of death.

Horwood absconded, but was apprehended Wednesday evening by several officers, but not without
making a desperate resistance, one of the officers being beat in a dreadful manner. — Yesterday he
was taken to the Infirmary, in order that the unfortunate girl might identify him, and appear to be
being the man; after which he was lodged in our Bridewell, preparatory to his being committed to
Gloucester Goal.——The unfortunate victim expired on Saturday Night, at the Infirmary, and a
Coroner's inquest will be held this day (Monday).

Harry Bonner, Printer, Bristol.

Newspaper report of Eliza's Balsom's murder

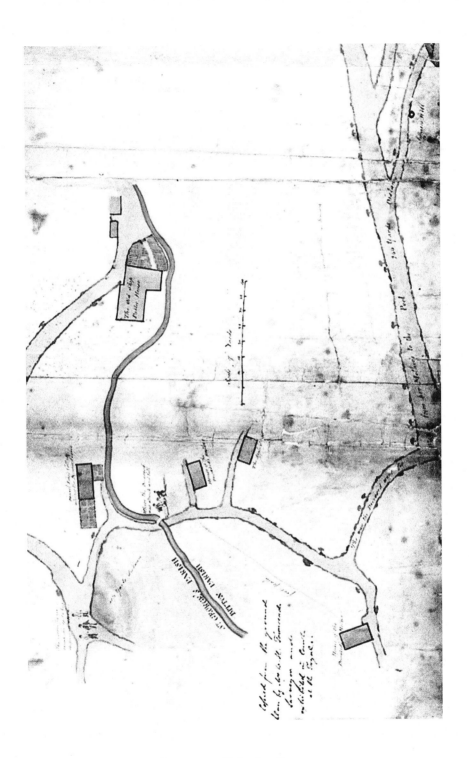

Drawing of Murder Scene

Rev. Robert Roberts, Methodist minister, and his prison pass

against him. The Reverend was trying to express to the accused the need to make peace with God, because if found guilty Horwood was sure to be executed.

The trial was set for Wednesday 11th April. Gentle words did not seem to impress the accused man, so on Friday 6th April the Reverend Roberts tried another approach in preparing his soul to meet God. He looked at his watch, looked at Horwood and said, 'today is Friday, two o'clock. By this time next week, your soul will either be in heaven or hell.'

Horwood seemed stunned and in shock. 'Do you think so, Sir?' he replied. 'I do, I believe you will not be on this earth' said the Reverend. Horwood now seemed more serious and attentive than before and seemed at last to understand the awful and perilous situation he was in. He turned to God, prayed and asked for forgiveness.

John Horwood was 17 years old when he was charged with Eliza's murder. The 10th April was his 18th birthday. Instead of celebrating his birthday with family and friends as a free man he was locked up, spending his time in prayer. He was probably reflecting on the tragic loss of his beloved Eliza and his own fate in court the next day.

# CHAPTER FOUR

## *Trial and conviction*

**From the Bristol Mirror, 14th April 1821:**

*On Saturday the 7th April between five and six o'clock, our worthy Recorder, Sir Robert Gifford, arrived in this City, attended by the usual cavalcade and proceeded to the Guildhall, where he opened his commission. On Sunday he attended Divine Service at the Chapel of St Mark, accompanied by the Body Corporate, an excellent sermon was preached on the occasion by the Rev. Walter Gray, from Isaiah, chapter xi x 9. The business of the Assizes commenced on Monday. The calendar was unusually heavy, containing names of no less than seventy three prisoners.*

With so many prisoners awaiting trial, the judge did not intend to spend any more time than was absolutely necessary on each case. The Spring Assizes began on Monday 9th April at the Star Inn, North Fleet Street, Bedminster. The trial of John Horwood was scheduled to begin some time on the Wednesday and after the last case on Tuesday it was announced that the trial would commence at eight the following day.

Wednesday came and the room at the Star Inn set aside for the trial was full to capacity with family, friends and the curious, long before the scheduled time of commencement. The prisoner was held in the lockup waiting the arrival of the judge. By eight o'clock the jury had taken their places, all was ready to begin the trial and the prisoner was brought up to the dock. The judge took his place and after the prisoner had confirmed his name the charge against him was read out.

'John Horwood, you stand here today on the charge of the wilful murder of Eliza Balsom. How do you plead?

'Not guilty' was his reply.

Messrs Gunning and Bumpus represented the Crown and Messrs Smith and Broderipp the defendant. The trial began - the King against John Horwood for Felony and Murder.

**The indictment stated:**

*John Horwood, labourer, of the Parish of Bitton in the County of Gloucester, to have put the fear of God before his eyes but being moved at the investigation of the Dear Oak\* on the Nineteenth Day of February in the Second year of the Sovereign George the Fourth of the United Kingdom of Great Britton and Ireland-King.*

*John Horwood hath with force and arms at the Parish of Bitton in the County of Gloucester aforesaid in and upon said Eliza Balsom against the Peace of God and our said Lord the King has there and then Feloniously Wilfully and of his Malice aforesaid swearing an Oath and that the said John Horwood swore she was of no value which to the said John Horwood in his right hand held a stone and there had cast it against and upon the right side of the head near the right temple causing a mortal wound and there Feloniously Wilfully and of his Malice did cast a stone and that the said John Horwood with Forethought cast the stone aforesaid as aforesaid cast and struck the aforesaid Eliza Balsom in and upon the right side of the head near the right temple of her the said Eliza Balsom then and there Feloniously Wilfully and of his Malice and Aforethought did strike penetrate and wound giving the said Eliza Balsom by the casting and throwing of the stone aforesaid in and upon the right side of the head near the right temple of her the said Eliza Balsom one mortal wound of the length one inch and the depth of one inch of which the said mortal wound of the said Eliza Balsom from the said Twenty Second day of January in the second year aforesaid until the Seventeenth day of February in the second year of aforesaid appeared as well at the Parish of Bitton aforesaid in the County of Gloucester aforesaid and also at the Parish of Saint James in the City of Bristol and County of the same City did languish and languishing did have on which said Seventeenth day of February in the said second year of the Reign of the said Lord the King the said Eliza Balsom at the Infirmary in the Parish of Saint James in the said City of Bristol and County of the same City of the mortal wound did die so say the Jurors aforesaid which they aforesaid do say that the said John Horwood killed Eliza Balsom in Murderous and with Forethought aforesaid Feloniously Wilfully and of his Malice aforesaid did Kill and Murder against the Peace of me the said Lord the King his Crown and Dignity."*

*(The Oak\* (Quercus Robur) is deeply connected in our hearts as representing the very essence of England and especially the power of the High King and his ancient and spiritual link to the land)*

**The prosecution began its case:**

*The prisoner at the bar, John Horwood, is charged with the Wilful Murder of Eliza Balsom, who was a young woman of about eighteen years of age residing with her mother a poor widow who is resident in the Parish of Hanham in this County and near the place where the prisoner lived. The prisoner had for a considerable time before the murder of the deceased plotted to gain an advantage over her affections, at least to have a relationship with her. The deceased regularly refused to keep company with the prisoner and refused him on every occasion until he threatened to murder her. The prisoner threatened to destroy her at one time on the*

*26th December last and threw a bottle of Vitriol over her clothes burning them, she ran away at that time to her mothers house. The conduct pursued by the prisoner, making threats, at different times, made it clear, his intent to commit the murder for which he now stands here. At one time the witness Rogers heard him swearing and threatening the deceased mother claiming, he be dammed if I don't kill her when I meet up with her again. Rogers was frightful to open his door as he had also been threatened by the prisoner, that he would knock his brains out. On the same evening the deceased was heard by her mother to say, for God's sake let me in, John Horwood is going to kill me, the mother looking out of the window saw the prisoner who swore he would smash her bones to pieces.*

*The following evening while the deceased was returning home in company with witnesses William Waddy and Joseph Reece she had reason to cross a brook at the bottom of some rising ground on which the prisoner was stood with two or three other men. The prisoner saw the deceased and watched her as she crossed the brook and threw something out of his hand and in consequence the deceased fell forwards into the brook and exclaimed, Ho I have been killed. She was taken to the infirmary the following day and advised by Mr. Richard Smith the surgeon who was attending to her to become an in-patient and Dr. Smith considering her condition called a consultation of the surgeons of the house resulting in him performing a trepan application it was discovered that a quantity of matter had formed on the brain. On the Saturday the 17th February the deceased died in the infirmary and Mr. Smith the surgeon states that the, effects of the stone was the immediate cause of her death. He also states that she was a virgin, this will be material as it is understood the prisoner has given out she was a common prostitute. The prisoner no doubt will try to prove he did not throw the stone as he previously denied throwing it in his examination.*

*The deceased in her disposition taken while in her death bed in the infirmary in the presence of the prisoner, swore that she saw him a short distance from her, that he swore at her and said he would kill her and commenced to take up the stone and flung it at her. The witness Barnes saw the prisoners arm move as if throwing and was denied by the prisoner from mentioning it at the time, saying not to mention what he had seen. The prisoner again threatened Barnes, don't tell a soul about the stone, a short time after this Barnes was met by the prisoner who supposing he had said something about throwing the stone, called him a deluded son of a bitch and threatened that that if he said any more about it he would be the death of him or not live long afterwards. This in itself is enough to show that Barnes knew of the prisoner throwing the stone, but there is another conjecture, Barnes was heard by Samuel Fry, to say to Horwood, it was a shame. The witness William Waddy who was with the deceased at the time the stone was thrown states that the prisoner said if he heard the deceased say it was him who threw the stone he would knock her bloody head off.*

*You will also hear in evidence of William Fry who was in company with Horwood at the time he threw the stone that he saw the arm of the prisoner as if he had thrown something and that he had something in his right hand previous to moving his arm and afterwards heard deceased cry out, Ho Lord I am dead. The witness Ann Fry swears that she has previously heard the prisoner say he would be the death of the deceased, if she did not keep company with him. These facts it is trusted to be sufficient to convince the Court and Jury that the prisoner at the Bar was the murderer of the deceased and he can't deny the statements of the deceased herself and the evidence of the witnesses Ann Fry, Thomas Barnes, William Woody and William Fry there is no doubt he will receive that punishment which the law points out. The examination is a direct result of the whole of the evidence addressed against him. He denied throwing the stone but says he was present when some other person flung* at the deceased. He denies throwing any Vitriol over the deceased this fact has been sworn by the witness Ann Fry and the deceased herself. He also denies ever threatening the deceased's life this as been sworn by three or four different witnesses. The conduct of the prisoner towards the officials who apprehended him only tends to strengthen the case against him. The officer Bull received a blow from a sledge hammer over his eye from the prisoner trying to knock him down if he had succeeded, he no doubt would have fled from the spot. There is another circumstance against the prisoner after the deceased was admitted to the infirmary he was heard to say, that if ever she came out alive he would murder her. It may also be proper to inform you that the young men in Hanham Cockroad are from a young age of childhood, in the habit of flinging stones at targets at forty to fifty yards distance and rarely missing one in ten. The following proofs of the evidence against the prisoner by the witnesses will show the mind of the prisoner against the deceased.

**Witnesses for the Prosecution were called
(Q = question, R = response)**

*Fry: I am Samuel Fry and live in Hanham.*

*Q: Did you see Eliza Balsom?*

*R: No, she was down the hill about 30 to 40 yards from the place we stood.*

*Q: Where was the prisoner?*

*R: On the brow of the hill.*

*Q: What happened next?*

*R: I heard a girl cry out, Ho I am killed, and I heard Barnes say, it was a shame. But I did not know what he meant.*

*Q: What were Barnes exact words?*

*R: It's a bloody shame.*

Q: *Who was Barnes talking to?*

R: *No one in particular.*

Q: *Did you see Eliza, was it her who said, Ho I am Killed?*

R: *I saw Eliza running up the hill a minute afterwards, but did not know who said, Ho I am killed. I went to see what had happened and found Eliza.*

Q: *You say you saw Eliza running up the hill, so you knew it was Eliza?*

R: *I did not know it was Eliza, it was starlight.*

The Judge intervened:

You have just said you saw her running up the hill, did you recognize Eliza?

R: *No, I looked towards the brook, but saw nothing.*

Q: *Where did the cry come from?*

R: *The brook.*

Q: *Was it a steep hill?*

R: *No, it was not steep where we stood.*

*Thomas Barnes will prove that witness knows the prisoner John Horwood and knew the deceased Eliza Balsom - That on or about the 21st day of January - That witness was standing at Hanham talking with the prisoner, Samuel Fry and William Fry about half past 7 o'clock in the evening - That witness saw the prisoner raise up as if he had thrown a stone or something out of his hand - Witness did not see anything thrown - Witness saw someone fall down near the brook at the bottom of some rising ground where Horwood was standing - The distance of the brook was about thirty to forty yards from the place Horwood was standing - That the prisoner denied witness not to mention his name - Not to tell of what he had seen done - That he again said, Don't tell about having the stone. That a few days after witness saw the prisoner who called him a deluding son of a bitch and threatened if he said any more about it he would be the death of him or that witness would not live long afterwards- That the conversation between them was about the deceased Eliza Balsom.*

### Call Thomas Barnes.

*I am Thomas Barnes a seaman on leave from the Navy. On the 26th January I was standing at the Four Cross-Roads at Hanham, Samuel Fry and John Horwood were with me.*

Q: *What time was it?*

R: *About eight in the evening.*

Q: *Could you see clearly, was it a bright night?*

R: *It was starlight.*

Q: *How far was the brook from where you were stood?*

R: *About 37 to 40 yards.*

Q: *Is there a crossing point over the brook?*

R: *Yes, there is a public footpath across it.*

Q: *Where were you stood?*

R: *We were stood on the hill above.*

Q: *What happened next?*

R: *I saw that young man [the prisoner] wave his arm (here he described the act of throwing)*

Q: *Did you see anything in his hand?*

R: *I saw nothing in the prisoners hand at the time.*

Q: *What happened after you saw the prisoner throw?*

R: *In the twinkling of an eye I heard someone fall down and a splash.*

Q:  Did the prisoner say anything to you?

R:  About ten minutes afterwards he told me not to speak of it.

Q:  Did you say anything when you heard the splash?

R:  I said, there's someone knocked down in the bottom.

Q:  Did the prisoner hear you say that?

R:  I said it loud enough for the prisoner to hear.

Q  Has the prisoner made threats against you?

R:  A week afterwards I saw him and he called me a, deluding son of a bitch for mentioning what I had seen. Another time he challenged me to fight.

Q:  Did you see Eliza after you heard the splash?

R:  I looked towards the brook but could see nobody.

Q:  Did you hear a scream?

R:  I heard a cry or scream of a woman and could distinguish the words, Ho Lord.

Q:  What was the prisoner doing and did you say anything to him?

R:  He was looking towards the brook and I said to him, it's a shame you have knocked someone down in the bottom.

Q:  Are you absolutely sure you did not see a stone in the prisoners hand?

R:  I saw no stone in his hand.

Q:  After the prisoner threatened you and challenged you to fight, did you part on good terms?

R:  I bore him no ill will.

William Fry - Will prove that on or about the 1st day of February last - Witness was in company with the prisoner, Samuel Fry, and Thomas Barnes at the time and place stated by them in their impositions - That *witness saw the prisoners arm, up, as if he had thrown something - That witness did not see any stone thrown - But saw something in the prisoners right hand previous to him moving his arm - That witness immediately heard someone shout out, Ho Lord I am dead. That witness went to see who it was and that it was the deceased Eliza Balsom - That the deceased then went home and the prisoner went up the hill.*

### Call William Fry.

*I am William Fry. I was with the prisoner that night. I saw her walk out of a neighbour's house walking towards her home.*

Q: *How far away from the house where you when you saw her?*

R: *About fifty yards.*

Q: *Did you hear her cry out?*

R: *She cried, Ho Lord.*

Q: *Where was she when she cried out?*

R: *Crossing the stream.*

Q: *Did you or anyone else go to assist?*

R: *I went down and saw it was Eliza some others who were further away than me also came.*

Q: *Did you know who it was before you went down?*

R: *No.*

Q: *Did you hear prisoner say anything to Barnes?*

R: *No and I was nearer to him than Barnes.*

Q: *When Eliza came out of the house did you know it was her?*

R: *I did not know who it was.*

Q: *Whose house did she come out of?*

R: *Dan Reece's.*

*Joseph Reece - Will prove that on or about the 8th day of February last he was in company with the deceased Eliza Balsom - That William Waddy was the farthest - That they were crossing a brook under some rising ground where the prisoner Horwood and three or four other were standing when the deceased Eliza Balsom received a blow from a stone - That witness believed was thrown by Horwood and fell into the brook. Witness got her out and she walked to her brother Richard Balsom's house - She complained of pain in her head - That at the time the stone was thrown Horwood and the other persons were about thirty to forty yards from the brook - That on seeing the prisoner the next day witness told him the girl was very bad and the prisoner said, he was sorry for it and that the stone was thrown, at about 8 or 9 o'clock in the evening.*

## Call Joseph Reece.

*I am Joseph Reece aged 14 years. I was with Eliza and William Waddy when she was hit by the stone. We were crossing the brook, I went first, William Waddy next and Eliza last. At the moment she was struck I heard a hum through the air, after being struck she cried out Ho Lord.*

Q:  Did you see who threw the stone?

R:  No, but I saw four or five persons on the hill, the prisoner was one of them.

Q: Y    ou say you recognized the prisoner, was it not too dark?

R:  There was enough light to see his face, he was looking towards the brook.

Q:  What was the colour of the prisoner's clothes?

R:  I could not tell it was too dark.

Q:  Have you spoken to the prisoner since?

R:  I saw him the next day and told him Eliza was very bad, he said he was very sorry for it.

*William Waddy - Will prove that on or about the 1st day of February last - Witness was going with the witness Joseph Reece to buy some apples - The deceased Eliza Balsom joined them, that whilst crossing the brook the witness heard a stone whiz by him and immediately the deceased fell into the brook - That the deceased received an injury on her head from the same stone, that the prisoner Horwood was near the spot. That witness has since seen the prisoner who said to witness, that if he was to hear the deceased say it was he who through the stone, he would crack her bloody nose.*

### Call William Waddy.

*I am William Waddy. I was with Eliza Balsom and Joseph Reece we were crossing the brook when Eliza was hit on the head with something. I don't know from which direction it came but it, hit Eliza and as she fell pulling me with her into the water and onto the stones in the bottom.*

*Q: Did you see the prisoner?*

*R: Yes he was with some others, about forty yards away.*

*Q: Did you assist her?*

*R: Yes, I went with her to her brother's house.*

*Q: Have you spoken with the prisoner since?*

*R: I saw him the same evening, I told him someone had said he threw the stone, he replied, if the girl said so, he would crack her bloody nose.*

*Ann Fry will prove that on Tuesday the 26th day of December last - Witness was in company with the deceased Eliza Balsom at a public house - That prisoner Horwood was there - Horwood took out a bottle of Vitriol from his pocket which he said he would throw over that common prostitute, the deceased and that he would not throw it over witness. That upon them going away the prisoner followed them and threw the Vitriol over them and burnt both their clothes. That witness had frequently heard the prisoner say he would be the death of the deceased because she refused to keep company with him.*

### Call Ann Fry.

*I am Ann Fry. I was at Eliza's brother's house when she came with her head cut and walked home with her after her brother dressed the cut. About three months before this happened I heard the prisoner, Horwood, say that if he saw her with another man, he would be the death of her. At Christmas I was at a public house with Eliza, John Horwood and some others. Eliza and John were very friendly at this time and I saw the prisoner pull a bottle out and heard him say, this is what I have to fling over Eliza Balsom.*

*Q: You say they were on friendly terms that night, how friendly?*
*R: I saw them dancing together and on very good terms.*

*Sarah Balsom - Will confirm that witness was mother to the deceased Eliza Balsom - That the deceased was about 18 years of age - That her daughter had for sometime under fright from the conduct of how the prisoner treated her - That on Wednesday the 21st day of January last between 8 and 9 o'clock in the evening, was in bed and heard her daughter shouting, for Gods sake mother let me in, John Horwood, is going to kill me, open the door. Witness jumped out of bed and her son let the deceased in. Witness opened the closed window and saw the prisoner Horwood and asked him why he used her girl in that manner, Horwood said, he would dash her bones too pieces and abused witness. That the deceased was always afraid to keep company with the prisoner and avoided him on every occasion.*

### Call Sarah Balsom

*I am Sarah Balsom mother of the deceased - The night she came home with her head cut, I cannot remember the exact day, but it was towards the end of January, between eight and nine o'clock. I was in my bed at the time and got up. My daughter's head was cut and very bruised, on the right side over her eye. The eye on that side was black, she was sick and vomited, continuing all the time. I dressed her head with bread and milk poultice. About five days after I took her to the infirmary. On Christmas night Eliza came home at about nine o'clock, I heard someone running fast, then I heard her cry out, mother open the door and let me in for John Horwood is going to burn me all to pieces. I heard him threatening, he said, the first time he caught her he would mash her bones all to pieces. I put my head out of the window and asked why he threatened my child that way. Horwood swore by his maker, that he would kill her and those that did take her part.*

*The Judge asked: Are you certain the person was the prisoner, did you see him?*

*R:   No, I did not go out, but I could tell it was him by his voice.*

*Mrs Balsom continued.*

*The Tuesday following, my daughter came home with something like grease all over her clothes, next morning they were all in holes.*
*Samuel Rogers - Will prove that witness is a labourer residing in Hanham in the County of Gloucester - That witness knows the prisoner and knew the deceased Eliza Balsom. That on or about Wednesday 21st day of January last witness was sitting by the fire in his own home with his wife and heard some argument. Witness did not open the door, the windows and door being shut. Being* fearful to do so as he had been threatened by the prisoner previous. That he would settle his brains out - Witness knew that the prisoner was outside and heard him shouting, I'll be damned if I don't kill thee when I meet with thee again. That the deceased mother lived next door to witness - That *the deceased at the time loudly calling to her mother to let her into the*

house - That this was between 7 and 8 o'clock in the evening. That it was the evening before Eliza Balsom received the blow.

### Call Samuel Rogers.

I am Samuel Rogers and lived next door to Mrs Balsom and corroborated the testimony she had given on the night the prisoner chased Eliza home. I heard Mrs. Balsom say she would get a warrant for him, to that he answered, you may fetch a warrant and be damned - I also heard him say, the first he met her, he would bash every bone in her body. He threw several stones into my garden.

Q:  How did you know it was Horwood?
R:  By his voice.
Q:  Did you go out to him?
R:  I did not, I was afraid the prisoner would knock my brains out.

Samuel Wilmot, alias Brooks, was called to give his evidence. A few days before he was apprehended, I was talking with the prisoner two or three others were present. I told him he could be tried and perhaps hang, he replied if she does not die there [infirmary] when she comes out, I'll be dammed if I don't kill her.

Q:  Was the prisoner drunk when he said it?
R:  Prisoner was not drunk.
Q:  Are you sure he was not in drink?
R:  He had no money for drink and had no drink.
Q:  So he was sober?
R:  He was quite sober.

Richard Smith - Will prove that witness is a surgeon of the Bristol Infirmary, that witness attended the deceased Eliza Balsom on or about the 31st January last as an outpatient of the infirmary in consequence of an injury or blow she had received in the right side of her head - That *witness upon consulting her immediately advised her to become an inpatient and she accordingly came in - That a consultation of the surgeons of the house was held on her case and after a necessary operation it was discovered that a quantity of matter had formed on her brain and that she has since deceased - That the injury or blow on her head and the matter there formed were the immediate cause of death of the said Eliza Balsom - That the said Eliza Balsom was a virgin.*

### Call Richard Smith.

*I am Dr Richard Smith the senior surgeon at the Bristol Royal Infirmary. Eliza Balsom was admitted to the hospital on the 31st January. She had a wound above the right temple, big enough to admit the top of a finger. The bone was bare and the outer table of the skull pressed inwards. Dr. Hetling (surgeon) happened to be there and we consulted upon what was best to be done. All of the surgeons saw Eliza on their daily rounds and she went on well for some time, after she fell off. It was determined on the 10th February in consultation with all five surgeons present, that the patient should undergo an operation that I immediately performed. It justified the opinion of the consultation, the girl having been relieved by the escape of a quantity of matter on the removal of a portion of bone. However, bad symptoms recurred, she languished until the 17th February and then died. I personally examined her body on behalf of the Coroner's Inquest, on the 19th. I found extensive inflammation reaching from the injured part to the substance of the brain, where there was a large abscess. The injury to the head produced the inflammation, the inflammation the abscess and the abscess, death.*

*The Judge asked what caused her death.*

R:  *The cause of death was the stone that caused the injury the injury caused the inflammation, the inflammation the abscess and the abscess death.*

*Q: What would be the symptoms?*

*Dr Smith replied that to an ordinary observer, the symptoms of injury to the head were vomiting, restlessness, stupor and the inability to do anything well, in proportion to the extent of the injury. There would be no saying when a patient was out of danger, as bad and even fatal symptoms could come on at all stages of the case. Concussion could produce all the effects mentioned, without the infliction of any wound. The functions of the brain are often deranged, with blows and falls, without any disorganization being apparent until examination after death. The skull might be compared to a thin book the two covers might represent the two tables and the leaves the intervening substance so that an indentation of the outer table did not necessarily make a pressure upon the brain.*

*The defence asked if the application of the poultices of bread and milk, salt butter and elder ointment applied by Eliza's family had been prejudicial in her death.*

*Dr Smith thought it had no bearing on her death:*

*I am not in the smallest doubt that the injury above the temple was the primary cause of all the subsequent mischief and that the abscess was the immediate cause of the girl's death.*

*The defence then asked what he thought caused the injury.*

*R: The wound appeared to be inflicted with a stone or some other blunt instrument.*

*Q: Would carrying heavy burdens on the head be with such an injury dangerous?*

*R: After such an injury, carrying heavy burdens on the head was very injurious.*

*Sarah Chapman - Will prove that witness is a nurse at the Bristol*

*Infirmary - That the deceased Eliza Balsom became an inpatient on or about the 31st January last and died at eight o'clock in the afternoon of Saturday the 17th February last - That the deceased before and after she had given her examination before a magistrate concerning the conduct of the prisoner told witness that she would not recover and wished to be sent home to her mother to die at home.*

### Call Sarah Chapman.

*I am Sarah Chapman, a nurse at Bristol Royal Infirmary. On the first day Eliza came to the house [the infirmary] she said she would die. She continued in that apprehension until her death. I told her she was in the hands of the Lord. She said she knew it and hoped the Lord would make him suffer [the prisoner] as she had done.*

*Mr Henry Day - Will prove that he was present at the infirmary in the Parish of St James in this City on Thursday the 15th day of February last and did then and there see the deceased Eliza Balsom, sign and subscribe her mark to a certain examination of her, the said Eliza Balsom and produced by witness before John Haythorne Esquire, one of his Majesties Justices of the Peace in and for the said City of Bristol and County of the same City - That the said examination read over to the deceased in the presence of the said John Haythorne and of witness and the deceased being sworn to the truth, also that the said prisoner John Horwood was present at the time the examination of the deceased was taken.*

*The examination of Eliza Balsom a patient in the Bristol Infirmary taken on oath in the presence John Horwood the 15th day of February in the year of our Lord 1821 before me John Haythorne Esquire, Justice of the Peace.*

*The informant on her oath said that she has known the prisoner John Horwood who has lived near the inpatients mother at Hanham in the County of Gloucester the last ten years. That the said John Horwood, had frequently made indelicate and improper proposals. The inpatient had constantly refused to yield to his solicitations and in consequence John Horwood had several times threatened to murder the inpatient. About Christmas last he had met and flung Vitriol over the inpatient or some other liquid burning the inpatient's clothes. Waylaid the in-patient with the intent to kill her. Towards the end of January last while walking in a lane at Hanham he got within a yard of her, the inpatient ran home and alerted her family who came out and he ran away. The following evening at eight or nine o'clock while walking with a person whose name she cannot recollect at present, the inpatient saw Horwood a short distance from her, he swore at her and said he would kill the inpatient, took up a stone and flung it at the inpatient, it struck inpatient on the head causing the inpatient to fall down and can recollect nothing else.*

*Also to prove the following examination of the prisoner John Horwood - Taken 15th day of February in the year of our Lord 1821 before John Haythorne Esquire.*

*The examinant said he was innocent of the flinging of the stone at Eliza Balsom. That he was present when some other person flung at her Samuel Fry, William Fry and Thomas Barnes were with him the time the stone was flung. Has known Eliza Balsom ever since he has been living. Never flung any vitriol over her and never threatened her life.*

After the deposition of Sarah Balsom and the examination of John Horwood, taken by Mr. John Haythorne Esquire Justice of the Peace, had been read to the Court by Mr Henry Day, this concluded the evidence of the prosecution. The Judge asked the prisoner if he wished to say anything. He replied 'I leave my defence to my councillors.'

### The defence then put their case:

*The prisoner John Horwood was committed to gaol on the 19th February last on the Coroners Inquest Charged with the Wilful Murder of Eliza*

Balsom. Before we proceed to state the circumstances attaining to this unfortunate transaction we beg leave to observe that the prisoner could have had no intention to murder the deceased as his being on the ground from where the prosecutions say he threw the stone was accidental.

John Horwood is a labouring man eighteen years of age or thereabouts and son of Thomas Horwood of the Hamlet of Hanham in the Parish of Bitton in the County of Gloucester. The latter has been in the employ of Mr Henry George and his predecessors Spelter Manufacturers for upwards of thirty years and is a careful and industrious man and respectable in his institution. The deceased was the daughter of Sarah Balsom and resident in a cottage near the residence of the prisoner's father in the same Parish and County within a short distance of the place where the accident the subject of this prosecution happened.

It has been for twenty years past usual and customary for the boys and girls of the above Parish also the adjoining Parish of St. George to meet together most nights on the ground where the prisoner and those with him were standing at the time the stone was thrown and how it was, the prisoner and associates were there on the night of the accident in question will appear by the following statement. On Wednesday the 17th or 24th January last the prisoner, Thomas Barnes, and William Fry met accidentally about eight o'clock in the evening, near the Ship Public House situated in the Parish of St. George in the County of Gloucester. They had not been there long before their attention was called to the singing of some girls who were a little before or in front of the prisoner and his companions and on their running towards the girls they ran away and the prisoner and his companions stopped on the ground the girls had just quitted and stood there talking. From which place the stone is said to have been thrown by the prisoner a distance of forty and a half yards from the place the deceased was at the time she was hit.

*Council's attention is now drawn to a plan and description of the ground in order to understand this case. The prisoner and companions walked from the Ship Public House in a westerly direction and on arriving on the spot were the stone was thrown they were in the Parish of St George and faced south and south east with a valley in front and stood in the following order - Samuel Fry on the right of the prisoner, Thomas Barnes on his left and William Fry next to Samuel Fry. East of the prisoner and his associates standing as described, in the bottom or valley is a cottage occupied by Daniel Reece, in the cottage the deceased was in the night she was struck by a stone. A rivulet or stream of water runs in front of this cottage and divides the Parish of St. George from the Hamlet of Hanham and the Parish of Bitton, both of these places are in the County of Gloucester, so Reece's cottage is in the Parish of St. George. Joseph Reece son of Daniel and William Waddy were in the same cottage with the deceased. The boys said to the deceased they were going to buy apples. Deceased said she would go with them so far on her way home and they all left together. Whether one or both the boys had crossed the rivulet situated about nine yards from the cottage is not certain, though believed the deceased, being last was in the act of crossing when something struck her. She grasped the boy Waddy who was close in front and fell with him into the said rivulet, she climbed out and afterwards got up without assistance and ran to her brother's house, up an assent about eight yards, crying she was killed.*

*The brother cut the hair off the wound with a pair of scissors and then shaved it and afterwards applied a plaster. The wound was about half as long as a man's thumbnail and the deceased was not faint or much alarmed. The deceased brother's house is in the Hamlet of Hanham and Parish of Bitton. The prisoner and his associates hearing a noise in the valley, Samuel Fry and the prisoner descended the hill and walked to the gate or entrance to the court in front of the deceased brother's house and* inquired what was the matter. Some of the boys standing around observed someone had thrown a stone and struck Eliza Balsom but no one knew who it was and it is remarkable and requires particular attention that when the prisoner and Fry reached the gate or entrance of the court to the deceased brother's house, that very second John Screach alias Bull and Rogers also made their appearance. They must have approached from a northerly direction or from the ground south west of the deceased brother's house. A stone thrown from the south or south west would have no doubt struck the deceased where she was hit.

At their meeting at the court leading to the deceased brother's house John Screach alias Bull said to the prisoner, some person has thrown a stone at Eliza Balsom and it will be said – It's thee as sure as thee's got an head. Prisoner said how could, they say it was him more than being Bull. Prisoner continued there about five minutes and then went away with Fry leaving Bull behind. As they walked southward up the hill on their way home the prisoner observed a man some little distance higher up on the brow of the hill and that he disappeared almost instantaneously he observed to Fry. Who is that there, Fry replied he did not know. The night was dark but not so much so that a cap might be seen by the prisoner and his associates as she crossed over or in the act of crossing over the brook. She did not have a hat on at the time and supposing a stone to have been thrown from the south or southwest side of the valley the deceased must have met it, but from where the prisoner and his associates stood as they faced the southeast it must have struck her in a oblique direction if she was in the act of crossing the rivulet as her back must have been towards the prisoner and his associates.

One of the boys who was walking with the deceased observed he could not say whether she looked round or not, but seemed to think the stone was thrown from where the prisoner and his associates were standing having observed men in white smock frocks. After the wound had been dressed with as we are informed a plaster of salt butter the deceased returned home and the following day continued her work as usual in cleaning her mother's house and fetching water and the like.

The morning after the accident a girl of the name of Hester Wall called on the deceased about eight o'clock in the morning and asked if she was going on the hill for water, to a well called Jeffery's Well a distance from the deceased house of two hundred and forty four yards. She said yes and went and returned together, the deceased filled her tub and afterwards carried it on her head home with apparent ease, the weight of the whole not less than fifty-six pounds and did it several times before she had to require medical attention either at the infirmary or somewhere. It appears by an entry in the books at the Bristol Infirmary that the deceased sought treatment on the 30th January and admitted as a in patient on the Tuesday 31st, seven or fourteen days after the accident had taken place. Supposing it happened on the 24th January due to the ignorance of the people great difficulty will arise in ascertain the exact day the stone was thrown. The solicitors on the part of the prisoner after much trouble and investigation are not satisfied on which day it was whether Wednesday the 17th or 24th January last. Not only during this time but after she had been taken into the infirmary, when escape was certain, the prisoner not only remained at home but came to Bristol for the purpose of getting a pig, with one Fry and on that occasion spoke with the deceased mother in Stokes Croft. These circumstances are stated as an attempt which we make to prove that the throwing of the stone was not an act of the prisoner and that, it is said, in consequence of attestations previously formed and on instances previous to the 17th January which were made by the declaration of the prisoner to do for the deceased. How far these declarations can be proved we can't say but if an attempt is made the circumstances attaining them must be well considered. *The prisoner no doubt loved the deceased and he has admitted that when they were together courting he has said to her, if thee don't let alone my ears I will kill thee, the deceased at the time pulling his ears. He declares he never threatened her life or offered to hit her brains out and that she told many lies about him.*

"It has been reported that the prisoner threw Vitriol on the deceased, but it is not true. *The prisoner and deceased were very familiar on the night, it will be shown that on or about the 1st January last that the prisoner and others spent an evening together at a house of one Martha Jones, that the deceased and another girl about four in the morning left Martha Jones house and accompanied her son on the road as far as the new church, about one mile, on his way to seek work in Wales, that the deceased afterwards returned alone to Mrs Jones cottage and found the prisoner there alone residing on a seat in the corner of the chimney, that she sat beside him and complained of the cold, saying she must have part of his coat, he had to cover him, which he gave her and on complaining a second time, he gave her more and at last the whole of it and after being together this way until seven in the morning, they both went home.*

*Up to this time the deceased could have no apprehension for her safety. The deceased was about the prisoner's age and it is supposed from the enquiries made that she was of gay and volatile disposition and that other persons will have had an improper intercourse with her but whether this was really the case we can't say and from what we have heard the girl must have been virtuous as Richard Smith Esquire one of the surgeons at the Bristol Infirmary examined the body and will prove it.*

*Thomas Bull assisted by others apprehended the prisoner at his father's house on the 15th February in the following manner, prisoner's father had left the cottage to go to his work about seven in the morning and his mother an old woman and ill in bed, the front door was on the latch and* a married sister named Catherine from an adjoining cottage was there assisting with the household work. The officers arrived and asked for John Horwood and on attempting to open the staircase door, which led to the prisoner's bedroom, the married sister alone below stairs refused them going up and placed herself against the door and demanded a sight of the warrant, saying her brother should come down if they wanted him but where was the warrant?

Without producing the warrant they removed her with some degree of violence and she says they presented a pistol to her ear and said do you see this? No warrant was produced and in this way they ascended the staircase which terminates immediately into the prisoner's bedroom and the prosecutors will say the prisoner most resolutely defended himself at the top of the staircase with a large hammer which he had in his right hand, but being overpowered was at last driven into his mother's bedroom, there he was secured. The hammer in question, if the prisoner had it, belonged to and was made for children of two or three years old to play with and would be produced, but a young child has since thrown it into a well and if it is possible to get it, but which we doubt, from the depth of the water, it will be produced in court.

Several severe blows were exchanged and the prisoner suffered from one of them, to which he was attended a considerable time by a surgeon. The prisoner was afterwards conveyed to the Bristol Infirmary where the deceased was pronounced to be in danger. He was near the deceased's bed at the time the information was taken and sworn by her afterwards before Mr Day magistrate and on the prisoner being informed of the contents of it he declared it was not true. He was asked when just brought to the deceased bedside what he had to say, he replied, of his horror of the sufferings of the young woman and declared his innocence. Whether a trepan operation of the wound in the head of the deceased made her *capable of giving a proper account of the accident Council will be pleased to consider.*

*The conduct observed by the prisoner at the infirmary has been represented as extremely callous. He is said to have been 28 years old and many other reports have been reported in common printed papers and otherwise leading to prejudice and inflaming the minds of the public, a circumstance people to be noticed on the trial as it has had the desired effect and the man in the eyes of the public is already convicted.*

*He speaks most solemnly that he felt for the sufferings and shed tears when he saw her in bed and made frequent inquiries after her by means of Mary Bees and offered to visit her while in the infirmary, which was declined. After being taken he was accompanied by his unmarried sister Mary and Ann Burnhill, the officers asked him how he came to do it - was it out of malice? His reply was he did not do it. His conduct in the gaol has also been the subject of observation and a report says a visitor observed to him his time would be short, he replied that he did not care how soon, for he was weary of being locked up in this place. This like many other aspirations had been improperly construed. What the poor fellow meant, was he wished to be well satisfied of his acquittal and liberty.*

*The principle witness on the part of the prosecution is Thomas Barnes, who is a seaman in the navy and some years since had a brother transported or its said. At the time of the accident he had lately returned from sea having received a considerable sum for wages and prize money and sailors like to drink for days and weeks together. Shortly after the accident the prisoner heard that Barnes should say he threw the stone. He immediately went in search of him and met by the Ship Public House and asked him, if he had said he, Horwood, had thrown the stone. Barnes said, do you wish to know? Prisoner repeated the question and received a like answer, upon which the prisoner said, do you wish to take my life and that Barnes should say one way or the other? Prisoner then offered to fight Barnes. He declined unless the prisoner would fight for money. The prisoner replied he had no money, but would fight for a belly full and began to take off his clothes, upon which Barnes said he would do him about the girl. Whether we shall be able to prove the circumstance, we can't say and it's probable Barnes would deny it.*

*The prisoner and Barnes afterwards were on bad terms and Barnes informed the deceased mother that Horwood threw the stone. The inquest was held on 19th February last at the Full Moon Public House in Stokes Croft, Bristol, and Barnes, Reece, Waddy and others were examined as witnesses. They were in attendance a considerable time previous to the Coroner and Jury meeting. They passed the time by enjoying themselves with smoking and drinking beer, so much that Barnes is said to have become rather intoxicated and it's certain he got up dancing, declaring he did not care for any man living.*

*Since his examination he has stated he barely knows the nature of the evidence he had given. The defence will produce proof of the age from Baptism Registers of the prisoner.*

*The defence witnesses were then called to give their evidence.*

*Hester Wall: This witness called on the deceased at her house about 8 o'clock the morning after the accident took place and asked if she was going on the hill for water. Deceased said she was and took a tub that would hold at least five and a half gallons of water. They walked together to the well. On their way there witness asked the deceased how her head was. She said not very sore because it was freshly done and that her mother told her there was but one cut, she thought there were two and that she did not know who did it. Witness and the deceased dipped their water and both returned together with the water on their heads. Deceased did not complain, but while at the well fell out and abused her sister in* law. The language used by her on the occasion is not fit to be mentioned. Witness left her at her mother's door and had no conversation with her until the following Sunday when she called at Hester Ainsbury's house, a neighbour, and saw deceased there in company with Martha Hudd. She then told witness her head pained her.

## Call Hester Wall.

I am Hester Wall. The day after Eliza was injured she saw her carrying water from a well in a tub that could hold six gallons. It had five and a half gallons in it and she carried it all the way home on her head. I asked how her head was and she said it's not bad.

Hester Hobbs spinster of the Parish of St. George: Witness went to a well called Jeffries Well on the Thursday morning after the accident happened for water and saw the deceased with her head tied up. Witness asked the deceased what was the matter with her head. Deceased replied some person cut it last night. Witness then said if she was in the deceased place she would fetch a warrant, upon which deceased said she did not know who did it, for three or four of them were standing together. She had a large tub or vessel for the purpose of carrying water. Witness went away and left deceased at the well.

## Call Hester Hobbs.

I am Hester Hobbs. The day after the accident she saw Eliza at Jefferies Well. I told her to get a warrant, she said she would if she knew which of them had thrown it, but there were three or four of them.

Q: How do you know this was the day after she was injured?

R: Because I was told so by the prisoner's father.

Jeremiah Bevan and John Oddy, the first a Methodist local preacher and the other a poor man but honest. Both will swear that for the last twenty years boys and girls have met on the ground where the stone was *thrown after work to amuse themselves and state the boundaries of the respective Parishes.*

*John Bull, alias Screach: To prove shortly after the accident the prisoner hearing Barnes should say he (prisoner) threw the stone went in search of and met him by the Ship Public House. Asked him if he had said he threw the stone. Barnes said do you want to know? Prisoner repeated the question and received a likewise answer. Prisoner said do you want to take my life? Barnes says one way or another. Prisoner offered to fight Barnes. He declined the combat unless prisoner would fight for money. Prisoner said he had no money but would fight for a belly full and began to take off his clothes upon which Barnes said that he would do for him over the girl.*

*Martha Hudd: Witness was with the deceased the whole of the following Sunday after the accident. They walked about three miles together. Witness asked deceased if she knew who did it. Deceased said she did not know.*

### Call Martha Hudd.

*I am Martha Hudd. Eliza came to her mother's house, the day before she went to the infirmary. I walked with her for three miles, through bye lanes from nine in the morning till nine at night.*

Q: *Where you together all the time?*

R: *Yes except at one o'clock when we separated for our dinner.*

Q: *You say you walked for three miles, was it dark?*

R: *Yes we walked in the dark.*

Q: *Was Eliza feeling poorly?*

R: *She was quite well, she never complained*

Q: *When did you hear she went to the infirmary?*

R: *The next day.*

Mary Bees - Witness will prove she went to the infirmary at the request of the prisoner- Asked the deceased if she had any objection to his coming to see her, which she declined saying she would rather give him a dose of poison. That witness was at the Ship Public House the day after Christmas till 3 o'clock in the morning. The prisoner and the deceased danced together- That she saw no Vitriol and if it had been produced she should on seeing it discovered it have been Vitriol.

### Call Mary Bees.

I am Mary Bees- Witness that there was a party at the Ship public house the day after Christmas when the prisoner danced with Eliza and they were very friendly and kind to each other.

Martha Jones, an old woman residing in the Hamlet of Hanham: The deceased and other girls and boys spent the 1st day of January in the present year at my cottage. The cottage is small consisting of two rooms. The old woman retired to rest in the upstairs room, leaving the young people in the room below, where they remained together until Eliza Balsom accompanied her son, who was going to Wales as far as St George's Church about one mile. Afterwards she returned to the prisoner who was still at the cottage. Prisoner and deceased reclined together in the corner of the chimney. The fire was out and prisoner behaved with kindness towards the deceased. Readily parted with his great coat to keep her warm. That he was very much attached to the deceased and loved her too much to hurt her.

Martha Jones was poorly on the day of the trial and could not attend.

William Jones - The son of the last witness will prove that the prisoner and several others together with the deceased were at his mother's house on the 1st January last. Deceased with another girl accompanied witness so far as the New Church on my way to look for work in Wales.

**Call William Jones.**

I am William Jones. Was at the party at the Ship and corroborate the evidence of Mary Bees.

**Sarah Balsom was recalled to the stand.**

Q: Was your daughter out and about the day before she went to the infirmary?

R: I was at home that day and Eliza never went further than the barton [garden].

Q: So she was either in the house or garden that day and nowhere else?

R: She might have been out three quarters of an hour at a time.

Q: What time did she get up and go to bed?

R: She got up that morning at nine o'clock and she went to bed early.

Q: Did she eat her breakfast?

R: She did not eat her breakfast that day.

Q: Did she see Martha Hudd that day?

R: No, she saw nothing of Martha Hudd.

Q: Did she go to Jefferies Well?

R: She did not go to Jefferies Well.

**Hester Balsom, sister of the deceased, was sworn.**

Q: Do you remember the day before Eliza went to the infirmary?

R: Yes.

Q: Did Eliza go out that day?

R: Eliza was at home all day.

Q: Did she go out at all?

R: She did not go out except to our Aunt's to get her head dressed.

Q: What time did Eliza go to bed?

R: Around half past seven.

Q: Did Eliza see Martha Hudd?

R: She never saw Martha Hudd. She did not come to see Eliza.

The Jury had now heard all the witnesses' evidence and the judge summed up the evidence for them in a most impartial manner. He made a special point of explaining the law; that if a person threw a stone with the intent only to inflict a partial mischief and death ensued, the crime would be murder.

At ten to four the jury retired to consider its verdict. The prisoner and his family had only a short wait; the Jury returned with its verdict at ten minutes past five. The judge returned and the prisoner was brought back up to the dock.

The court clerk, Frederick Collier Cooksworthy, asked the jury foreman if they had reached a verdict. 'We have' he replied. 'How do you find the defendant, guilty or not guilty?' asked the clerk. The foreman replied, 'Guilty.'

During the whole trial the prisoner had paid great attention to all the evidence without betraying the slightest emotion. When the verdict was announced he shed a few tears and put his handkerchief to his face twice.

The Judge put on his black cap and addressed the prisoner.

'I have observed that after a severe and painful investigation, you have been found guilty of wilful murder and of murder under very aggravated circumstances. You were instigated to the crime by the refusal of the young woman to yield to your improper solicitations and the necessity to restrain your passions, which you did not, that have brought you to the Bar were you now stand. I conjure you to prepare yourself for the presence of that judge to whom the secrets of all hearts are known.'

The Judge, in a faltering voice and almost overwhelmed by the intensity of his feelings, pronounced the sentence.

'John Horwood, you are convicted of the wilful murder of Eliza Balsom. You shall be hanged by the neck until you shall be dead on Friday the 13th April instant and your body be delivered to Mr Richard Smith, of the City of Bristol, Surgeon, to be dissected and anatomized.'

Immediately after the sentence the prisoner was hurriedly removed from the court into the waiting coach and under heavy guard escorted from Bedminster to the New Prison at Bristol.

Later in the evening Rev. Roberts visited Horwood in his prison cell. The prisoner, feeling the effects of standing in the witness box all day, was showing signs of tiredness. After discussing the outcome of the trial with him and a few prayers, he left him to rest, promising to return in the morning.

# CHAPTER FIVE

## *Last rites*

The defence council had without doubt failed to put a strong case in favour of their client. Their opening account concerning the circumstances of the case against him was nothing more than a long-drawn-out, rambling speech, that probably sent the jury to sleep.

In all probability John Horwood did throw the stone, but a stone thrown a distance of forty yards on a moonless night with only starlight to see by is such an uncertain method of murder it could scarcely count at all. He was in company of witnesses, and it would be unlikely he would attempt murder under those circumstances. No barrister should have missed the chance in that direction. There was no attempt to procure mitigating circumstances in an appeal against the death sentence, although it is known that among the populace there was a strong feeling in favour of the convicted man and a belief that he had not been an intentional murderer. The guilty verdict has the sense of propriety, of repaying like with like and taking the life of one who has taken the life of another.

His parents were devastated by the outcome of the trial. After discussing their options between themselves, they sought further legal advice. On the Thursday morning at a meeting with their solicitors, they were advised nothing could be done under British law regarding the outcome of the trial. They decided to appeal directly to Dr Smith, to release the body to them so that they could hold a Christian funeral, instead of him dissecting it. The following letter was sent to Dr Richard Smith.

### To Richard Smith Esq. Bristol 12th April 1821

*Sir.*

*Having been concerned, as solicitors, for the unfortunate man, John Horwood, who will expiate his offence tomorrow and commiserating the agonized state of his aged father and mother, we venture to express a hope and earnestly solicit your kind interference, in obtaining a remission of that part of the sentence which relates to the dissection of his body. The restoration of which would tend, in a great degree, to tranquillize the minds of his unfortunate parents. We therefore felt it our duty (with the conviction that you would give the case your kind and serious consideration) to make this application on their behalf.*

*We are Sir, your most obedient humble servants.*
*Browne and Watson.*

A reply was received on the Friday morning.

### To Messrs Browne and Watson Solicitors.

*Gentlemen. Infirmary 13th April 1821.*

*I have submitted your application respecting the body of John Horwood to my Brothers (surgeons) and after very serious consideration of all the circumstances of the case we have come to a painful resolution that, consistently with duty which we owe our fellow citizens as Public Officers, we cannot comply with your request. I assure you that we commiserate very truly the mental sufferings of the friends of the unhappy Criminal and regret exceedingly the necessity of the refusal. For myself and Brothers, Gentlemen, I remain your most obedient Servant.*

*Richard Smith*

Another letter was sent, this time pleading for what ever was left of the body after dissection to be released to the family for Christian Burial.

### Broad Street, Friday 13th April 1821.

*Sir.*

*We have been favoured with an answer to our letter on behalf of yourself and Brethren. Although we cannot help feeling how strongly you regret the circumstances which prevent your compliance with the last and only wish which can be granted to the unfortunate parents of John Horwood, we shall further beg permission to Public Officers, since justice towards the Public is satisfied. The present application therefore is still further to solicit the indulgence of the request, the granting of which will under any restrictions, be most gratefully received and acknowledged by the distressed Family for whom we have been concerned.*

*We are your obedient Servants.*
*Browne and Watson.*

An immediate reply was given.

### To Messrs Browne and Watson. 13th April 1821.

*Gentlemen.*

*I have placed before the surgeons of the infirmary your second Letter, respecting the Body of John Horwood. We have in consequence reconsidered the matter in the most serious and deliberate manner and I am under the unpleasant necessity of saying that we can see no reason for altering the opinion expressed to you in my former communication. The father and brother of the unfortunate malefactor have probably informed you, that I have had with them, at my house this morning a most painful interview and certainly, if I had permitted my feelings to have assumed the mastery over my sense of duty in this miserable affair,* the tears of so respectable an old man would, as far as I am personally concerned, have prevailed and forced me to yield to his solicitations.

I trust however, that even this afflicted parent went away satisfied with the rectitude of the motives which alone actuated the surgeons and convinced that they were prevented from being free agents by due sense of the obligations due from them to their fellow citizens.

I need scarcely, Gentlemen, point out to you, although that I alone am named in the Order of the Court, yet I consider myself in trust for my brethren conjointly and that I do not feel at liberty to act without their concurrence.

Allow me also to observe that an attentive and unprejudiced consideration of the wording of the Warrant of the Sheriffs and the guarded receipt to me imperative as to the fulfilment of the latter part of the sentence. It is, as you know, not merely for dissection that it was delivered to me by the Magistracy, but to be anatomized, the real meaning and intent of which can scarcely be misunderstood. How far the body might be given up for internment, I shall not take time upon me to determine (although it must be concluded, that the Act of Parliament is very strongly featured) yet, after the obligation incurred by the conditional Receipt given to Mr Oddy Hare, the Under Sheriff, I cannot but feel myself morally bound to complete its intention.

It is therefore clear to me that after having given to the Professional Students of Bristol and to as many Gentlemen as may please to honour me with their presence, a summary course of Lectures, that Remains ought to be formed into a skeleton and deposited by the side of two unfortunate Infanticides, who after execution were delivered to the late Mr Godfrey Lowe, for the same purpose a few years since.

The Surgeons, Gentlemen, feel fully satisfied that you have, on your part done your duty in your strenuous endeavors to alleviate the mental *sufferings of your client and they I trust, that in return, you will give them credit for acting upon no other principles than these which ought to actuate all persons holding public situations.*

*I Remain, Gentlemen.*
*Your, most obedient Servant.*
*Richard Smith.*

From Smith's letter it seems Thomas, the father of the condemned man, accompanied by his son Joseph, had visited Dr Smith at his house on the Friday just hours before the execution in a personal final plea for the release of the remains of his son after death and whatever was left of the body after the doctor had finished cutting it up in public so that he could give him a Christian burial. Smith refused. His letter clearly states that the bones of the skeleton would be all that would be left and that they should be placed with the skeletons of the two women executed for child murder 20 years earlier.

On the Thursday morning the Reverend Roberts returned as he had promised to the prisoner and found him more composed, and they sat down to converse on the consequences of sin. Rev. Roberts adopted a very plain style as he found it difficult to find comparisons to suit Horwood's understanding. He asked him if he knew what was meant by Christ dying for sinners. Had he ever heard of Christ? Horwood replied that he had heard something of him. Rev. Roberts continued with him until two o'clock, when he left after his family had arrived to say their last farewell.

John's father Thomas, accompanied by his daughter Mary and son Joseph, went to the prison to visit the condemned John for the last time on this earth. His mother was confined to bed with sickness. This account by Rev Day, Prison Chaplin, gives his eyewitness account of their last meeting with their beloved son and brother.

We were conducted to the prison chapel; after waiting about five minutes, I heard the faint rattling of chains; and looking towards a narrow passage that led to the chapel, I saw the unfortunate Horwood, conducted by a turnkey from his cell, with his irons and prison cap on. This was an awful sight to see. As he advanced towards us, I perceived he could not look up; his countenance bespoke the anguish of his heart. Before he came up to where we were, his sister sprang towards him, fell upon his neck and with a piercing and bitter cry, exclaimed, 'O my dear Brother! O my dear Brother! O my dear Brother!' Her heart was too full, to say anything else; and his was too deeply affected to make her any reply. She repeated her exclamation many times, before sinking to her knees exhausted. Then the poor grey-headed Father approached him in a like manner, fell upon his neck and was so filled with grief and sorrow, that it was some time before he could speak: at length he broke out, 'O my dear son! What to die tomorrow! O my son! My son! O my dear son!'

In about five minutes the poor old father sat down quite overcome. Then his brother, Joseph, saluted him, and wept and lamented over him; after they were a little more calm and collected, we seated ourselves on the form with the unfortunate young man and we engaged in prayer. He was besought to look to Jesus. He said, 'Oh Sir, I am a guilty sinner.' 'Jesus Christ came into the world to save sinners,' was the reply. He said, 'but do you think he came to save me?' 'yes; you are the very character.' At this assurance, a ray of hope appeared to dart across his face. 'My dear brother, there is mercy for you; Jesus, died for the vilest of the vile; God accepts of a broken and contrite heart; and believe me, if you cry earnestly to the Lord for mercy, he will show it to you, and enable you to rejoice in his salvation.'

His brother Joseph wept over him and exhorted him to prepare to meet his God. He told him that his time was short; that eternity was at hand; and that he must be born again, or he could not enter the kingdom of heaven. He was told by the Rev. 'to pray for himself, do pray for yourself, my dear brother, come now and begin and cry to God for mercy.' Immediately he broke forth in this manner, 'O Lord God, be merciful unto me, and forgive me my sins! O Lord, thou, knows, that tomorrow before one o'clock, I am to die. Lord save, my dear soul. Lord, have mercy upon me. I deserve to be in hell, but, O Lord, thou didst send Jesus Christ to die for poor sinners. O Lord, for Christ's sake, teach, me to pray, and show me thy mercy.' He seemed very much calmer and at peace with himself after he prayed.

As the clock struck three, he said, 'tomorrow by this time I hope, through God's mercy, to be at his right hand.' His father came to his side, in the deepest of grief and anxiety, fastened his eyes once more upon him, but could not speak; he squeezed his hand and bathed in tears; he placed his other hand on the unfortunate young man's head, stroking his hair. He exclaimed, 'O my dear son! Did I ever think I should be the means of bringing a child into the world to be hanged, O my son! O my dear son! Be much in prayer to God, and I hope he will show thee mercy.'

His dear sister came forward to him, her face filled with kindness and affection. He put his hand into his waistcoat pocket and took out three pence; placing the three pence into his left hand, and putting his right hand in his breeches pocket, he took from thence, a piece of paper folded together; he unfolded it and took out six pence; he put the six pence with the three pence and delivered both to his sister. This act overcame all present, after all he had done in this world; he seems to be conscious of it, he is bidding farewell to it, he is taking leave, he is giving up his all. His sister burst into a flood of tears and cried, 'O my dear brother! I shall never see thee again, O my dear brother! What to die tomorrow! O my dear brother! Thus she continued till a fit of hysterics came to her relief. The poor father flew upon his neck, and embracing him for the last time exclaimed 'O my son, my dear son! O my dear son! Continued for about five minutes and then sat down exhausted. His brother Joseph kissed him for the last time and reminded him to look to God for support in the coming trying hours.

Farewells over, Horwood was escorted by the turnkey through the iron railings. He stretched out his hand through the grating and shook hands for the last time with his father. Then he proceeded to his cell and the door was locked behind him.

Rev. Roberts returned at four o'clock, just as the visit was ending, and told them that John had opened his heart to God and a special service to celebrate his life and seek God's forgiveness. It was to be held at Jeffries Hill (Hanham) Sunday next and tents were to be erected to accommodate the large congregation expected to attend.

Rev. Roberts remained with John, most of the time spent in prayer. He said he was not afraid to die and hoped he would, by this time tomorrow, be in heaven with dear Eliza. At midnight he indicated that he wished to be alone, and the Reverend then left him to his own thoughts.

# CHAPTER SIX

## *A brave farewell*

The execution was scheduled for one o'clock and the spectators began to gather early in the morning to obtain the best viewing points. The authorities soon became concerned and posted notices of the danger to the onlookers getting too near and falling into the New Cut. This was the first hanging at the New Prison. The new scaffold had been constructed over a trap door on the flat roof over the main gate, by a local carpenter who had copied the one at Gloucester. He had charged £30 for his services.

By noon thousands had gathered to watch and the whole event had taken on a carnival atmosphere. Hawkers selling their wares did a roaring trade, as did local printers, who had produced news sheets telling the 'True Story of the Murder and Confession of John Horwood'.

The appointed executioner had arrived in good time to inspect the drop and make any adjustments to his satisfaction. Hanging at this time was not a quick process, as the long drop which used the victim's own weight to break his neck had not been invented. The short drop in use at this time was more like strangulation, and often did not provide a quick death.

The Methodist ministers visited Horwood early in the morning and told him of the service to be held at Jeffries Hill in his memory on Sunday. He said, 'Tell all my friends not to sin as I have done and to turn to God, lest they finish up like I have.' The ministers assured him they would do as he wished. They then 'exhorted him still steadily to look to Christ Jesus for hope and salvation; wishing him grace, mercy, and peace; in the awful moment of dissolution, we left him in the capable hands of the Rev. Roberts'.

Soon after this, he assembled with the other prisoners in the prison Chapel. Reverend Day, the Prison Chaplain, conducted a service, and at the end Horwood was invited to speak to the inmates. 'My fellow prisoners; I am about to die, although you told me I would not. I am not afraid; but, remember, it was sin that brought me to this; let me warn you to take me as an example. At eighteen years of age I lose my life through sin; and if you do not break off your bad habits, the end will be bad.' This address was delivered in 'so affecting a manner, that not a dry eye was to be seen among the whole assemblage, whether prisoner or other'.

Horwood then returned to his cell and remained alone for fifteen minutes. Reverend Roberts then went to him and found him in the same humble, composed state. They continued together till the Sheriff came with his warrant; when he entered he took Horwood by the hand, and was so affected that he could not for some time deliver the summons.

Horwood whispered to Roberts 'the time has come.' He then took his arm and walked to the Governor's rooms to thank him and his family for the kindness and attention they had shown him. They then went to the 'dead room' immediately under the drop, when for the last time they publicly engaged in prayer. Horwood prayed in an extremely striking manner, and the Sheriffs, Mr Humphries, and the officers were all bathed in tears. He shook hands with all those present and informed them he held no malice against them.

He ascended up to the platform in chains and leg irons and immediately stood on the door of the drop, raised his eyes to heaven, and, without once looking upon the surrounding multitude, appeared to be wholly engaged in prayer. After the executioner had adjusted everything to his liking there was a long and tense interval. This did not arise from any guilty fear, but because Horwood was absorbed in prayer. He did not seem to notice the passing time.

At about half past one Horwood let fall the handkerchief (this was the pre-arranged signal that he was ready to die) and he was launched into eternity. He seemed to die instantaneously.

According to the eyewitness account of Dr Richard Smith:

*I had been invited to breakfast that morning with one of the Sheriffs, Robert Jenkins, Esquire, who resided at the end house in Redcliff Parade. After breakfast Mr. William Oddy Hare, the Under Sheriff, called and we made our way to the prison. On arrival we were taken to the parlour of the Prison Governor, Mr. Humphries. There were about fifteen persons there, chiefly well dressed females. Shortly after, Horwood was brought in. Attended by half a dozen constables, he bowed awkwardly, and seemed to be suffering great mental agony. He looked around the room and said, 'pray for me, do pray for me, do pray for me!' This produced a sort of shriek of horror amongst the assemblage. They knelt down one after another and presently one female began to pray aloud, and by her manner and easy flow of words, I had no doubt that she had been accustomed to addressing an audience extemporaneously. Horwood remained standing, but listening with great attention and evidently accompanying the speaker mentally, but perfectly silent. This lasted about ten minutes, when the female, who seemed to be rather above ordinary class, but not a gentlewoman, ended and rose. Horwood then walked round the room and shook hands with all who presented themselves. I was not among that number, for obvious reasons, in fact I stood behind a person lest he might recognize me, and that having given evidence against him, and even my errand might flash across his mind. (he had come to collect his body). He wrung his hands and seemed in great distress and exclaimed, 'O Lord! O Lord!' The officers then stepped forward and bound him and he speedily left the room. The Reverend Day walked before him reading the burial service. Almost everyone was greatly affected, many shed tears, and I believe that I did not escape the contagion. The funeral service of the Church of England is at all times affecting, and under these circumstances its effect is irresistible to those who have feelings. I certainly felt at the moment an indescribable sensation of depression and lowness of spirits. I now went up the opposite stairs, which look down close upon the scaffold where the culprit was just arrived, but there was a great bustle and the impression was that there had been some resistance or attempt at escape, but I soon learned the cause. The fact was that the head of the executioner had failed him and he had slipped away and hid himself as soon as he observed the near approach of the criminal. After some searching he was found hiding behind a door and brought on to the scaffold. Horwood behaved very well, he appeared to be absorbed in prayer, the rope was adjusted and the people began to leave the platform, and my courage, if courage it is to be called, failed me. I perceived that the fatal moment was approaching and I was unable to look any longer at the criminal. I drew back almost involuntary, turned my face from the scaffold, walked back to the stairs, making my way to Mr. Humphries parlour. There I found a few of the females who had been there before and Sheriff Jenkins. A little later Mr Oddy Hare came in, bowed to the Sheriff and notified him officially that the criminal had suffered the sentence of the law. Soon after this Mr. Humphries came in and advised me to quit the jail at once, intimating that it would be impossible to do anything in regard to the body that evening or perhaps the following day. This was prudent advice as he had information that Horwood's friends, aided by a large number of colliers and stone-quarryers, had laid a plan for rescuing the body by rushing suddenly upon the escort; whilst some were fighting, others would get to the body and carry it to a waiting boat and rowed up to Hanham. If that should happen recovery would be beyond possibility.*

The Bristol Mirror of 14th April gave this account of Horwood's address to the other prisoners in the prison chapel in the service conducted by Mr Day on the morning before his execution:

*The prisoner acknowledged that the evidence upon which he had been convicted was true, that he knew it was Eliza Balsom who had been passing the brook and that he was waiting for her, at the time. Raising his hands towards Heaven, he added 'Lord thou knowest that I did not mean then to take her life, but merely to punish her, though I confess that I had made my mind up at sometime or another to murder her'. He also confessed that he had been guilty of several robberies and he should have thought more serious of his situation. This confession was not mentioned by either the Rev. Day or the Rev. Roberts, if there had been a confession it would have been made to one of these Gentlemen.*

The newspaper then gives an account of the execution:

*He kissed the hands of the prison officers, escorting him, ascended the platform in a firm step, even though in leg irons, he appeared calm and collected. The executioner removed the neck-cloth from round the prisoner's neck, placed the rope and adjusted it. A long and painful interval of suspense occurred. It was supposed by the spectators, that he was afraid of making the signal, but he was engaged in prayer for more than twenty minutes. He then spoke with Mr. Humphries, asking if he thought he would have much pain in dying and requesting him, if he should struggle, to put him out of his misery as quickly as possible. He began to pray again, but after a few minutes, at half past one, he dropped the handkerchief and was launched into eternity. He seemed to die instantaneously.*

*After the execution the Methodist ministers made their way to Hanham for the purpose of comforting his distressed parents and family. We found them surrounded by some pious neighbours who had come to condole with them. His mother had spent the whole of the previous night in prayer to God for him and in consequence, seemed much exhausted. We told her what had occurred during our visit with him that morning she appeared thankful and with great humanity, expressed her gratitude to God. We prayed with her and her family and informing her of our intention to fulfill the request of her unfortunate son by preaching on the adjoining hill the next Sabbath.*

Dr Smith found himself in a predicament. He had given a receipt for the body of John Horwood to the magistrates before the execution had taken place, so it was now up to him to collect the body from the prison. He devised a plan to get the body to the infirmary. Under normal circumstances the body would have been delivered to him by the prison authorities and in his possession directly after the extinction of life had been declared and the body taken down from the scaffold. The inhabitants of Hanham, in support of the mother and father of the executed, intended to hijack the escort at some place between the prison and the Bristol Infirmary, to prevent the second part of the sentence, dissection. On the Saturday morning Smith put his plan into action. According to his own account:

*I asked a coachman whom I knew, if he had any objection to go with me to the jail to fetch a parcel? 'Oh no Sir! I know what you mean!' I stepped into the coach and we drove to the jail. We were let into the courtyard. The body was in a room under the 'Drop,' and naked. I gathered up the ropes and cap. Mr. Humphries then sent some men and ordered them to put the body in the coach, but they one and all most peremptorily refused to go near it. Finding that his authority went for nothing, I betook myself to an argument that was irresistible, I showed two of the fellows a half-crown and assured them it would be theirs when Horwood was in the coach. One of them said to the other, 'come Tom, what dost say, come lay hold of him,' and they placed the body in the coach. I wrapped around the upper part of the body an old Irish cloak that it might not be seen through the windows, and pushed it into a corner. I was about to close the door when David Morgan, one of the Sheriffs Yeomen, said, 'Sir, would you like me to accompany you?' This opened my eyes to the awkward predicament in which I found myself, if the contents of the coach should be discovered during the transit. I therefore gladly accepted his offer. All being ready and orders given that no one was allowed leave but ourselves, the doors opened and we drove off at speed as fast as our cattle [horses] would allow. We passed the New Bridge, through Prince's Street, went up Marsh Street, crossed St. Stephen's Street, went into Christmas Street, and through Lewin's Mead to Earl Street where there was situated the lower door of the Infirmary. We met not the slightest interruption, from the men from Hanham. Upon arrival I jumped out and calling to some persons belonging to the Infirmary, the body was borne out of the vehicle. At this instant passed a soldier and a woman, both of whom appeared astonished, but passed on. I discharged the coach, and the whole affair was fortunately accomplished. The body was placed upon a trestle in the dead-house.'*

Smith had managed to outfox those seeking to prevent him getting Horwood's body. They were unaware he had it at the

Infirmary, because they hung about the streets of Bristol all Friday night and Saturday. It was Sunday before they realized that Smith had the body:

*A few hours before his dissolution, he expressed a wish to Ministers attending to him in his cell, that they would improve the awful circumstance, on Jeffries Hill, Hanham, where he was brought up and in the neighbourhood of which, the fatal occurrence took place for which he suffered.*

*This is therefore to give notice. That on Sunday next, April, the 15th, 1821, there will be three public Religious Services on the above mentioned JEFFRIES HILL. Two large tents will be erected for the occasion. The meetings will commence at Ten o'clock in the morning, Two o'clock in the afternoon and Half-past Five o'clock in the evening.*

*On Wednesday Evening next, at Seven o'clock the circumstance will be further improved at the PATHAY CHAPEL, by two of the Ministers who were present when Horwood made the above request.*

The tents were erected on the Saturday evening and all was ready in good time for the expected crowds the following morning. The weather on the Sabbath was favourable and about two thousand persons assembled; all of them seemed deeply affected. At the afternoon service a multitude attended, possibly as many as nine thousand. The weather was reasonable until the conclusion of the service and then a violent and long hailstorm greatly annoyed the congregation. The greater part had no umbrellas, but found shelter in the tents. The storm rendered the roads exceedingly unpleasant and no doubt prevented many from attending the evening service, however about two thousand three hundred were present.

On the Monday, 16th April, in the evening, Dr Smith gave a

public lecture to around eighty gentlemen, gentlewomen and students. No one who applied was refused entry and his wife was among the observers. In his lecture he demonstrated the circulation of the blood through the hearts of simple animals, reptiles, fish, birds and quadruples and then used Horwood's body to explain the flow of blood in the human body. On the Tuesday evening, again to a large attendance, he demonstrated the workings of the viscera of the abdomen. He then handed the body to his students. All who attended Smith's lectures were highly satisfied with the interesting and informative lecture, accompanied by a great number of beautiful drawing and anatomical preparations.

By this time the body was decomposing at a rapid rate and after the Thursday it had to be surrendered to nature, but before this Dr Smith had another use for it. Before the rotting flesh was removed from the bones and the bones reassembled into a skeleton, he carefully removed the skin from the flesh. It would have taken a lot of skill and patience to remove it in a large enough piece for its intended purpose - to bind a book.

Two of Bristol's sheriffs were tanners by trade, and they gave him advice on the process of treating it. After removing the skin from the body, the remaining traces of flesh and fat were removed by carefully scraping it with a blunt instrument until clean. A weak mixture of salty water, urine and oak bark was placed in a bath and the skin allowed to soak. The skin was turned two or three times a day and the solution increased in strength every four or five days. After six weeks the solution would be at full strength, and it was soaked for a further two weeks, being turned only twice a week, after which it was hung to dry gradually. Caution prevailed in not having the mixture too strong in the early soaking stages, otherwise there was the danger of contamination of the skin that would show up as dark marks and stains that could not be removed.

Smith followed their instructions and used a professional tanner to complete the process of turning the skin into cured leather fit for bookbinding. It was another seven years before he sent the skin to the bookbinder.

A receipt dated June 1828 for the sum of £1 10s (£1.50p) was for 'binding in the skin of John Horwood a variety of papers relating to him and letters engraved on each side of the book 'Cutis Vera Johannis Horwood".

A plaster cast of the head of John Horwood had been taken before dissection began and after the hair was shaved from his skull. A lot of interest was shown in the skull; most were curious to know if it had the characteristic bump which it was believed at that time that all murderers had. Two men from Germany who were on a visit to Bristol, experts in the relatively new medical field of phrenological research, were invited to examine the skull. Neither of them found the 'Bump of a Murderer', but a 'Phrenological Wheel' produced by one of them gave the chief characteristics of John Horwood to be 'combativeness, self-esteem and hope'.

The skull was kept at Dr Smith's house and he took great pride in showing it to friends and guests at every opportunity. In 1827, six years after the murder, Dr. Spurzheim and others dined at the house. After the ladies had left the table, Smith produced the skull and asked Dr Spurzheim, his opinion of it, without revealing any clue to the identity. Directly he saw it, he exclaimed, 'oh, brutal, brutal, manifestly brutal, it has all the animal propensities.'

Dr Spurzheim was a leading expert at the time in the study of phrenology - indeed he had created the term, to mean the study of the workings of the brain. He was born in Trier, Germany in 1776 and having studied the new science, gave lectures on the subject throughout Europe. He died in Boston, USA in 1832 from typhoid.

# BEWARE

## OF THE

# BANKS

### OF THE

# RIVER,

### AND

# THE BRIDGES.

HARX BRYAN AND CO CITY PRINTING OFFICE, BRISTOL.

Public notice posted on the day of execution

Sir Robert Gifford, the trial judge

1821

Bristol Gaol Delivery

The King

against

John Horwood

for Felony and Murder

Brief for the Prosecution

Indictment states that John Horwood late
of the Parish of Bitton in the County of Gloucester labourer not
the fear of God before his eyes but being moved and seduced by the
Instigation of the Devil on the ninth[?] day of _____
year of our Sovereign Lord George the Fourth _____
United Kingdom of Great Britain and Ireland King
faith with force and arms at the Parish of Bitton
the County Gloucester aforesaid in and upon one Eliza _____
the Peace of God and our said Lord the King then and there being
feloniously wilfully and of his Malice aforethought did make
an assault and that the said John Horwood _____
as valued which to the said John Horwood in his right
and there had and held in against and upon the _____
the head near the right temple _____
and there feloniously wilfully and of his _____
did cast and throw and that the said _____

Front page of Prosecution Indictment.

Bristol Gaol Delivery
7 April 1821

The King
against
John Horwood

Brief for Prisoner

& Indictment

## Case

The Prisoner John Horwood was Committed to Gaol on the 19th February last charged on the Coroners Inquest with the Wilful Murder of Eliza Balsum — before we proceed to State the Circumstances attending this unfortunate transaction we beg leave to observe that the Prisoner could have had no intention to Murder the Deceased as his being on the Ground (from whence the prosecutors say he threw the Stone) was accidental

The Prisoner John Horwood is a labouring Man 18 Years of Age or thereabout and Son of Thomas Horwood of the Hamlet of Hanham in the Parish of Bitton in the County of Gloucester — the latter has been in the Employ of Messrs. Harvey George & Comp. (and their Predecessors) Spelter Manufacturers upwards of 24 Years and is a careful Industrious Man and respectable in his situation — The Deceased was the Daughter of                    Balsum and resided in a Cottage near the residence of the Prisoners Father in the same Parish and County and within a short distance of the place where the accident the Subject of this Prosecution happened

It has been for these twenty Years past usual and Customary for the Boys and Girls of the above Parish and also of the adjoining Saint George to meet together most Nights (after leaving their work) on the Ground where the Prisoner and those with him were standing at the time the Stone was thrown and how it was that Prisoner and Associates were there, on the Night of the transaction in question will appear by the following Statement

On Wednesday the 17th or 21st January last The Prisoner James Fry. Thomas Barnes and William Fry met accidentally about 8 of the Clock in the Evening near a Public House called The Ship situate in the Parish of Saint George in the County of Gloucester they had not been there long, before their attention was called to the Singing of some Girls who were a little before or at some of the Prisoner and his Companions, on their running towards the Girls they ran away and the Prisoner and his Companions stopped on the   to

# THE LIFE,  & DEATH,

## OF

## JOHN HORWOOD,

Who was executed on the New Drop, at Bristol Goal, on Friday last, April 13, 1821, for the
wilful Murder of ELIZA BALSUM;—together with his Confession and last awful Moments.

On Friday morning, the last duties of religion were performed in the Gaol before John Horwood and his fellow-prisoners. The service of the Church was read by the Rev. S. DAY, who also preached an affecting Sermon, from Rom. chap. viii. the whole of the latter. The service was read at the particular request of Horwood. After the Sermon the unfortunate man addressed his fellow-prisoners, exhorting them to take warning from him, for that his sins had brought him to his present unhappy condition. He acknowledged that the Evidence upon which he had been convicted was true—that he knew it was Eliza Balsum who was passing the brook, and that he was waiting for her at the time. And, raising his hands and eyes towards Heaven, he added, "Lord! thou knowest that that I did not mean then to take away her life, but merely to punish her; though I confess that I had made up my mind, at some time or another to murder her!" He confessed also, that he had been guilty of several robberies; and that he should have thought more seriously about his situation, but that some of the Witnesses against him had, since his confinement, got up into the trees in the Rope-walk, close to the Gaol, and had thence given him to understand, that they would not say any thing that would do him harm on his trial.

He said that he ran away immediately after firing the stone. He had not been in the habit of attending any place of worship. He addressed himself particularly to the boy who had been convicted for setting fire to Mr. Horby's house, and seemed anxious to make an impression upon him.

The Rev. Mr. Roberts remained with the prisoner until ... on Thursday evening, when the prisoner ... ed a wish to be alone. The Rev. Gentleman ... visited him frequently during the last fortnight. He found him ignorant in the extreme, and evidently filled with the vain belief that he would be acquitted.

In a conversation with the Rev. Mr. Roberts on Thursday night, on the subject of death, he said he was not afraid to die; and he "hoped he should meet the dear girl in Heaven by that time to-morrow night."

Every preparation having been made for the Execution, the Sheriffs entered the Prisoner's cell at 10 minutes after 12 o'clock.

A short time before the prisoner was brought down, he expressed a wish to see the Keeper's family. One Lady fell upon her knees, and "hoped that God would forgive him." He added, "I hope he will."

He was then let out, at 10 minutes before one o'clock. It was evident to all present, that he was deeply engaged in prayer as he passed along. He was taken to the Dead Room, under the Drop, where he remained till 5 minutes past one, when the Clergyman left him.

At 10 minutes past 1 he ascended the platform; and as he passed the Officers, he kissed the hands of each, declaring that he bore no animosity to any one. He ascended the platform with a firm step; he even appeared calm and collected. The executioner having removed his neck-cloth, and adjusted the rope, a long and most painful interval of suspense occurred. It was supposed, by the spectators, that he was reluctant in making the signal; but he was engaged in prayer for more than 20 minutes; after which he spoke to Mr. Humphries, and asked him whether he thought he should have much pain in dying; and requested, if he struggled, to put him as quickly out of his misery as possible. He remained a few minutes more in prayer; and at half past one he was launched into eternity.——Horwood was 18 years of age on the day of his condemnation.

Hardy Bonner, Printer, Bristol.

Printed news sheet

# THE LIFE, CHARACTER, CONFESSION AND BEHAVIOUR OF
# JOHN HORWOOD,

*Who was Executed on the New Drop, at Bristol, on the 13th day of April, 1821, for the Wilful Murder of ELIZA BALSUM.*

I JOHN HORWOOD, the unhappy victim of depraved habits, that am now about to suffer the just sentence of the Law, in so ignominious a Death, was born in the Parish of Bitton, in the County of Glocester, of poor but honest parents, who endeavoured to rear me in the path of Virtue, but unfortunately for me I too much neglected their good advice; instead of going to Church on Sundays, I often went rambling about with wicked boys, and soon became hardened in vice; I was never shocked at the idea of committing any crime, untill the Judge passed the awful Sentence of Death upon me, for having been buoyed up by my companions in jail that I should get out of it, I never took it seriously to heart, and for the first time in my life, when the Judge passed Sentence of Death upon me, I began to repent of my Sins, and alas, without the interposition of a merciful SAVIOUR, it is much too late.

Early in life I contracted an intimacy with the young woman who was the victim of my cruel and barbarous passion; I had long kept her company and often wanted her to marry me, but she refused me in consequence of my bearing such a bad character, and so gave her company to another young man, at which I was so exasperated that I could not rest night or day, and I so gave way to jealousy that I often thought I would destroy her rather than she should go with any one else—I often told her that I would murder her if she did not leave off the other man's company, and

when I began to think of that I could scarcely think of any thing else; I haunted her about a long time to find an opportunity of putting my dreadful purpose in execution, till at last the devil worked me up to such a pitch that I could let her alone no longer, and I struck the dreadful blow which caused her death; but I hope the Almighty God has had mercy on her soul, and has received her into his Heavenly Kingdom, and that he will comfort her distressed and afflicted relations; and oh! how it grieves my bleeding heart to think that were she is I cannot go.

> But, Jesus, thou art all in all,
>   In mercy ever sure,
> Ready to help the vilest wretch,
>   As thou hast done before
> Pardon O Lord, from thee I crave,
>   For a whole life of sin,
> That e're I reach my silent grave,
>   I may feel grace within.

And now my fellow Sinners, and all who may witness my untimely end, I beseech you to let my fate be a warning to you, to resist the first temptations to vice, and whilst I beg you to join me in hearty prayer to the Almighty God, that he will send down his pardoning love to my soul before the breath leaves this mortal Body, I beseech you not to upbraid any of my relations with my disgraceful end. May the Lord have mercy upon my poor Soul. Amen.

BENNETT, PRINTER, QUAY-STREET, BRISTOL.

Another news sheet

# THE
# TRIAL & EXECUTION
### OF
# JOHN HORWOOD.
#### WHICH TOOK PLACE AT
# THE NEW CITY GOAL

This Day (Friday, April 13 1821,)

For the wilful Murder of ELIZA BALSAM, of HANHAM, near Bristol.

JOHN HORWOOD, aged only 18, was indicted upon the Coroner's inquest for the wilful murder of Eliza Balsam; who, as our readers may recollect, died at the Infirmary from a blow by a stone, supposed to be thrown by the prisoner. A number of witnesses were examined to prove the occurrence, the heads of which have already been laid before the public. Jos. Fry, Thos. Barnes, and Wm. Fry, were with the prisoner on a hill, near the spot; they did not see the prisoner throw a stone, but heard the deceased fall into the stream of water, and heard her exclaim, O Lord!——Barnes indeed swore, that he immediately said to the prisoner—"'Tis a shame, you have knocked some one down in the valley."—the pathway was about 50 yards from where they stood.

Jos. Reece was with the deceased, when she went to pass the brook, heard something hum in the air, which struck deceased on the right side of the head; she fell into the water, and exclaimed, "Oh, Lord;—was ultimately taken to her brother's house. Witness saw four or five persons on the hill, from whence the stone or whatever it was, came—Saw Prisoner amongst them, his face was towards them, the others backs.

Wm. Waddy was also with the deceased, heard the stone hum, deceased fell, and caught hold of him, and he fell also into the brook, there were stones in the brook for people to walk over, deceased fell on her left, the blow she received was on the right side of her head. Saw Prisoner same evening, after deceased was taken home—heard Prisoner say, if he was to hear her (deceased) "say, that he have the stone he would crack her bloody nose."

Hannah Fry assisted deceased to wash off the blood, &c. and helped to take her home.—Had heard Prisoner say, on a former occasion, "that if he caught E. Balsam with another man he would be the death of her"; saw him pull out a bottle and said that was what he had to fling over E. B.

Sarah Balsam, the mother, said, deceased came home on a Wednesday, between eight and nine o'clock, the latter end of January; witness was in bed, daughter was very ill, had a cut in her head, was sick and vomiting all night, dressed her head with a poultice, got worse, taken to the Infirmary 9 days after.—Witness knows prisoner, saw him about a week before; on Christmas night deceased came home, heard some one run very fast; deceased called out—"Mother, open the door, and let me in, John Horwood is going to burn me all to pieces." Heard prisoner on the outside, who said, "The first time I catch her I will mash her bones small as ashes, and d——d his bloody eyes. Witness bolted the door, looked through the chamber window, and asked prisoner why he threatened her daughter, he swore by his Maker that he would kill her, and those who took her part. The Tuesday night following deceased went out again, and came home with her clothes covered with something like grease, and they dropt all in holes next morning.

Samuel Rogers was the next sworn. Heard Prisoner say, the first time he met deceased he would be the death of her; heard him throw many stones into the barton after deceased took refuge in the house. —— Brooks deposed nearly to the same effect.

The Judge then summed up the evidence very fully; and the Jury having retired for about an hour, returned a verdict of GUILTY.—— The Judge then proceeded to pass sentence in a most solemn manner, putting on the fatal black cap, and ordered him for execution on Friday, and his body to be anatomised; on hearing of which the prisoner burst into tears.

This morning, pursuant to his sentence, the unhappy culprit underwent the awful sentence of the law.—Notwithstanding that indifference to his fate which he evinced during his trial, we understand that after he left the Court he became deeply affected.—Several Christian friends attended him and by their exhortations awakened in him a sense of his guilt and impressed him with a desire to seek for salvation by prayer at that Fountain of Mercy, whereby alone it can be attained.—On the platform he shewed great penitence, and after joining the Clergyman in prayer, the fatal signal was given, the Drop fell, and a few moments put an end to his earthly existence.

Harry Bonner, Printer, Bristol.

Another news sheet

The ruins of Prison Gate, the place of execution

Dr Smith posing with quill pen and skull

# John Horwood,

Executed at Bristol, April 13, 1821, for the Murder of Eliza Balsum by a blow from a stone which he threw at her. Part written in his lifetime, & when strongly impress'd with a most propitious issue, and part since his death, by a Fellow-Prisoner.

*Printed and sold by W. Collard, Bridewell-Lane, and Hotwells.*

My name it is John Horwood,
I was born at Hanham in the forest of Kingswood,
Vast numbers here do work in the coal-pits,
But for my part I always dreaded it ;
The line of life I adhered to then,
Was briefly that of a labouring man.
Whilst I did work upon a new line of road,
This awful thought oft times to me occur'd,
That its completion I should never live to see :
But then as little did I think 'twould be my lot,
To be first who suffer'd at Bristol new jail & drop.
To Eliza Balsum I then did make my suit,
But with the only view her person to pollute ;
For which she justly did with scorn me treat.
Murder her I told her I certainly would do,
And once I burning vitriol o'er her threw.
Always threat'ning her in language harsh & rude.
That sore in dread of me she & her parents always stood.
Returning from a friendly visit she had been to pay,
I treacherously did her way-lay,
And whilst she was crossing of a brook,
By the star-light my fatal aim I took.
O Lord ! some body has killed me she aloud did cry
At which I took to my heels and run away,
Threatening my companions I would beat,
If ever they discovered who did the deed.
To cure the wound I with the stone did make,
My victim they did to the Bristol infirmary take,
But symptoms appearing to grow worse and worse
Two officers well arm'd were for me dispatch'd,
With my road hammer one of 'em o'er the eye I cut
But to superior force compelled to submit,
Into her presence I was quickly brought,
That she my person might identify on oath :
Of those who heretofore murder had done,
Skeletons and 'otomies were to me shewn,
But I was not to be frightened by a box of bones.
Next to the jail they escorted me along,
And never more the rays of liberty upon me shone
One night whilst in my dreary cell I lay,
Methought I heard some friendly voices hailing me
Twas my companions had climb'd the tall trees,
Immediately in my prison's vicinity,
Cheer up, said they, as sure as ye're in iron apparel
Our evidence shall not harm you on the day of trial
I was for my rough spirit always reckon'd a crack
                                          chap,
Assuredly this did it revive like brandy drops,
With fancied liberty once more I grew so elate upon
I almost forgot I had the rivets on.
On the morn of the 11th of April, 1821,
At the awful bar I was arraigned,
And vain, alas ! all efforts here to save me prov'd,
The judge told me my case being of a nature such
That for pardon only in God's mercy I must trust
Then he the awful sentence nam'd,          [came,
John Horwood you must return from whence you
Which caused many a tender tear to flow,
From those who'd sons and daughters of their own

Sceleta
Johannis Harwood,
Qui (propter cædem
Hannæ Balsam commissam)
Laqueo Suspensus erat,
Die Veneris,
Idibus Aprilis,
Anno Domini
1821.

Rd Smith Esq
Park St.

Executed
Friday 13 April 1821

Skeleton
Johannis Harwood
homicidæ
propter Han. Balsam
cædem
ultimo supplicio
affecti.
or
Skeleton
Johannis Horwood
de patibulo suspens
of Han. Balsam
homicidium.

Received of Mr Richard Smith
three Guineas for articulating the skeleton
of John Horwood Joseph Cook
Decr 13th

Skeleton articulator
and receipt for three
Guinnesses

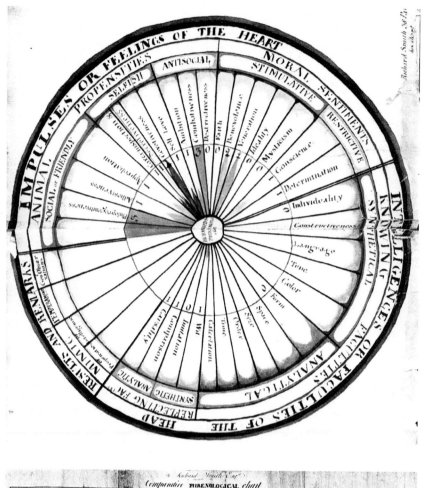

Phrenological wheel and chart

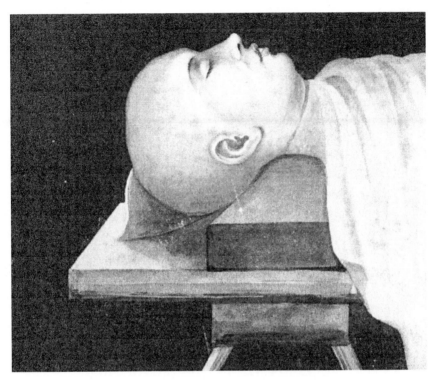

John Horwood's body in the infirmary dissecting room,
head shaved, awaiting Dr Richard Smith

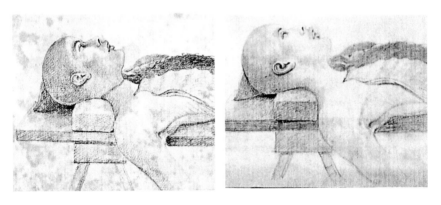

Sketches of John Horwood's body made during dissection

# The *DYING* Request

OF

# JOHN HORWOOD.

A few hours previous to his dissolution, he expressed a wish to some Ministers who were then present
with him in his Cell, that they would improve the
awful circumstance, on *Jefferies Hill*, Hanham,
where he was brought up; and in the neighbourhood of which, the fatal occurrence took place
for which he suffered.

## *This is therefore to give Notice,*

THAT ON

## SUNDAY NEXT, APRIL, the 15th, 1821,

There will be three public Religious Services on the above
mentioned Jefferies Hill.

## Two large Tents will be erected on the occasion.

*The Meetings will commence at Ten o'Clock in the Morning;*
*Two o'Clock in the Afternoon;*
*And Half-past Five o'Clock in the Evening.*

MR. THOMAS ROBERTS, Baptist Minister, who has paid
great attention to the unfortunate young man, will preach the
Evening Sermon, and give several interesting particulars concerning
him.

N. B. On Wednesday Evening next, at SEVEN o'Clock,
the circumstance will be further improved at the PITHAY
CHAPEL, by two of the Ministers who were present when
HORWOOD made the above request.

## \*\*\* *Please to tell your Neighbours.*

Rose, Printer, Broadmead, Bristol.

Methodist memorial service

# The DYING REQUEST of
# JOHN HORWOOD.

A few hours previous to his dissolution, he expressed a wish to some Ministers who were then present with him in the Cell, that they would improve the awful circumstance, on *Jefferies Hill*, Hanham, where he was brought up; and in the neighbourhood of which, the fatal occurrence took place for which he suffered.

*This is therefore to give notice,*

That on Sunday next, April, the 15th, 1821,

There will be three public Religious Services on the above mentioned

### JEFFERIES HILL.

Two large Tents will be erected on the occasion.

*The Meetings will commence at Ten o'Clock in the Morning ;*

*Two o'Clock in the Afternoon ;*

*And Half-past Five o'Clock in the Evening.*

On Wednesday Evening next, at Seven o'Clock, the circumstance will be further improved at the PITHAY CHAPEL, by two of the Ministers who were present when HORWOOD made the above request.

*The following Hymns will be sung on the occasion.*

### HYMN 1.

SERVANTS of sin attend ;
Why labour ye for death ?
And toil for an unhappy end ;
The wages from beneath.

Short is the longest thread
Of this our mortal state ;
Why hurry to the world of dead ?
Will sentence come too late ?

Why bid stern justice draw
The sword from out the sheath ?
Why, by a violated law,
Demand untimely death ?

Hear! Horwood speaks to you ;
Oh! hear him from his cell!
Just as he bid the world adieu,
Young Horwood wish'd you well.

Go, go, and warn, said he,
The wicked of their ways;
Tell them, Oh tell them, Sirs, from me,
Sin will cut off their days.

Go to that very spot
Where my companions dwell;
Oh! cry aloud, and spare them not:
Preach judgment, death, and hell.

Tell them, their crimes will lead
Where mine, alas! led me;
Who, number'd, now, among the dead,
Must hang upon the tree.

Hear then, poor sinners, hear!
Hear God's own awful word!
Oh! hearken, take good heed, and fear,
And turn unto the Lord.

Oh may his Spirit's power
Arrest the slaves of sin:
Oh may he in this gracious hour,
A mighty work begin.

May crime, and guilty death,
Be never heard of more;
But may we all with ransom'd breath,
A Saviour's grace adore.

---

## HYMN 2.

JUDGE of the earth! and God of power!
Behold the crowds assembled here:
Bow down thy heav'ns in this dread hour;
Thy judgments and thy truth declare.

While here we stand before thy face,
Trembling beneath our load of sin;
Oh! magnify thy pardoning grace,
Thy work of mercy, Lord, begin.

On him who bled on yonder tree,
Fix every eye, nail every heart;
And, while the crucified we see,
Force us with all our sins to part.

By our Redeemer's dying pains,
His bleeding hands, and feet, and side,
Oh! wash away our guilty stains;
Oh! cleanse us in the crimson tide.

Now, help thy servants, bless thy word,
Let sinners hear, and fear, and flee;
On each, on all, thy grace be pour'd,
For still there's mercy, Lord, with Thee.

## HYMN 3.

JESUS again we spread,
  For Thee, this humble shed:
Often have we seen Thee here,
Gaz'd on our Emmanuel's face;
Sunk, o'erwhelmed, with holy fear,
Lost in transport and amaze.

Again thy heav'ns bow,
  Oh! stoop and meet us now;
Let the cloud again descend,
Let it on the Tent appear;
Clad with glory, Israel's friend,
Come and tabernacle here.

Now let thine arm awake,
  The guilty earth to shake;
By thy lightnings fiercest dart,
Pierce the gloom of sin and hell;
Rend each rebel's rocky heart;
God of thunder, make them feel.

Then from thy mercy's seat,
  When humbled at thy feet,
Whisper pardon to the soul;
Calm the trembling sinner's fears;
Make the wounded spirit whole;
Wipe away the mourner's tears.

Our hallelujahs then,
  Shall rise to heav'n again;
Angel choirs shall hail the song,
All the first-born join our lays;
Wafting still our joys along,
Still extending Jesu's praise.

Till earth and heaven resound,
  All, all the lost are found;
Till from far those millions come,
Till from death those millions rise,
Till with joy returning home,
All the ransom'd reach the skies.

———  ———

## HYMN 4.

STOP, poor Sinner! stop, and think,
  Before you farther go:
Will you sport upon the brink
  Of everlasting woe?
Once again, I charge you,—stop!
For unless you warning take,
  Ere you are aware, you drop
    Into the burning lake.

Pale-fac'd Death will quickly come,
　To drag you to the bar;
Then, to hear your awful doom,
　Will fill you with despair;
All your sins will round you crowd;
Sins of a blood-crimson dye;
　Each for vengeance crying loud;
　And what can you reply?

Though your heart be made of steel,
　Your forehead lin'd with brass,
God at length will make you feel,
　He will not let you pass:
Sinners then in vain will call,
(Though they now despise his grace)
　Rocks and mountains, on us fall,
　And hide us from his face.

---

## HYMN 5.

SINNER! behold the Lamb!
　The bleeding Lamb of God'
Come, feel the music of his name,
　And taste that he is good.

On yonder cursed tree,
　His wounds were opened wide;
And there his blood was shed for thee,
　And there for thee he died.

O sinner, lift thine eye,
　Behold his grief and pain;
Oh! hear him groan, Oh! see him die;
　Thy sins the Lamb hath slain.

I see thy pity move,
　Thy tears are falling fast;
I see the Saviour's melting love,
　Hath broke thy heart at last.

Oh! prize those contrite tears,
　His grace to thee abounds;
Flow faster still; flow on thy tears;
　Mercy may yet be found.

Though foulest loads of sin
　Oppress thy guilty soul,
His blood can cleanse from every stain,
　His grace can make thee whole.

P. Rose, Printer, Bristol.

The Delivery of our Sovereign Lord the Kings Gaol in the City and County of Bristol of the Prisoners in the said Gaol being held in the Guildhall in and for the said City and County on Saturday the seventh April 1821 before George Hilhouse Esquire Mayor, Sir Robert Gifford Knight Recorder and others their Associates Justices assigned &c

John Horwood — Convicted of the Wilful Murder of "Eliza Balsum"

"Let him be hanged by the Neck "until he shall be dead on Friday the "thirteenth day of April instant and let "his body be delivered to Mr Richard Smith "of the City of Bristol Surgeon to be dissected "and anatomised"

Received this thirteenth day of April 1821 from Thomas Hassell and Robert Jenkins Esquires Sheriffs of the said City of Bristol and County of the same City the Body of the above named John Horwood deceased for the purposes mentioned in the above Trial or Sentence —

Richard Smith
Surgeon

Receipt given by Dr Richard Smith for the body

A TRUE AND PARTICULAR ACCOUNT OF

# AN ATTEMPT TO ROB

# BEDMINSTER

## Church-Yard,

## Of a Female Body,

Early this Morning, (Saturday, November 2, 1822,)

AND THE APPREHENSION OF

# FIVE OF THE

# DOCTORS.

Early this morning, Eight men, including several Doctors, entered the Church-yard of Bedminster, near Bristol, and began their nefarious work of plundering a grave wherein a body was interred on Sunday last, who had died at the Infirmary.—She was considered a fine *Subject*, and the Doctors were determined to have her at all events.—They had nearly succeeded in *raising the dead*, when Mr. Yates, of the Lamb Inn, and several other Constables, who perambulate the Streets of Bedminster, nightly, as Patroles, entered the Church-yard, and discovering what was going on, instantly seized five of the depredators, (the other three made their escape) together with the whole of the paraphernalia used for the occasion.—A desperate conflict, however, took place before they secured their prisoners, and one of the Doctors received so severe a wound that it was found necessary to send off for some of their *Fraternity*, to his assistance.—They were all taken to Mr. Yates's house, the Lamb Inn, where they now are, and it is expected they will undergo an examination before the Justices this Day.

E. Bonner, Printer, Castle Mill-Street, (Under Newgate) Bristol.

Bodysnatching notices and newspaper cuttings

Dr Smith, painting commissioned by the infirmary

# 50 Guineas
## REWARD.

### St. Augustine's Vestry Room,
MONDAY 25th October 1819.

**Whereas** on the Night of FRIDAY last, or early on SATURDAY Morning, the CHURCH-YARD of the Parish of St. AUGUSTINE was entered, and the CORPSE of a FEMALE, which had been interred on the preceding Morning, was TAKEN UP and STOLEN therefrom by some Persons unknown.

### THIS IS TO GIVE NOTICE,
THAT A REWARD OF

# FIFTY GUINEAS

Will be paid to any Person who shall give such Information as may lead to the Conviction of the Offenders the Vestry being determined to use every exertion to bring the Parties who have been guilty of an act so abhorrent to the feelings of human nature to Justice.

☞ The above Reward will be paid by Mr THOMAS URCH, Denmark-Street, the Churchwarden, on Conviction of any one or more of the Offenders. An Accomplice making a discovery will receive the same Reward.

### OSBORNE & WARD,
VESTRY CLERKS.

J. M. Gutch, Printer, 14 Small Street, Bristol.

NOTICE OF REWARD FOR APPREHENSION OF BODY-SNATCHERS.

Bodysnatching notices and newspaper cuttings

# APPREHENDING & TAKING

### OF

# Two Resurrection-Men,

#### Alias

# BODY-SNATCHERS

Who were detected this morning at 2 o'Clock, on Redcliff-Hill, with a DEAD CARCASS in a gig.

INFORMATION having been given to two of the
watchmen belonging to Redcliff-hill district last night, that a gig had left Bristol
late in the evening, in which were mounted two of the sons of Æsculapius, who
were strongly suspected of being out on a Resurrectional expedition, and a description of their persons and the gig being accurately given, the watchmen kept a sharp
look-out, but the lingering moments rolled slowly on, till " Past one o'clock" had
echoed loud on Avon's banks, and these " trusty guardians of the night" had almost
given up the hope of capturing those midnight marauders of the peaceful tomb,
when peeping o'er the bridge they descried, " by the light of the moon" the very identical
gig moving rapidly along; they immediately went towards the hill, on the summit of which
they stopped this travelling depository of the dead, and on searching, discovered that it
contained a corpse but very recently disinterred. The gentlemen were accommodated
for the remainder of the night in the watch house, and their dead companion was also deposited near them, also the apparatus with which they had taken it from its peaceful
mansion.——Reader! I doubt not but thou hast some relative consigned to the grave;
I would ask thee what thy feelings would be to see their remains taken from the mother
earth and manacled and cut to pieces merely to satisfy the curiosity of those who may call
themselves " gentlemen of the faculty," and argue that it is necessary and beneficial to
society? We have been informed that the body was taken from Backwell church yard,
and that the gentlemen are in custody.

E. Shepherd, Printer, Q. Broad Weir, Bristol.

Bodysnatching notices and newspaper cuttings

A Full and Particular Account of the

# DISINTERMENT

OF THE

# CORPSE

OF MRS. RICE,

## BY SOME RESURRECTION MEN,

On last night and the night before, with a farther Account of the manner in which the
Corpse was recovered by the Husband, when the Surgeons were in the act of

# DISSECTING IT.

ON Sunday evening last the body of Mrs. Rice was interred in St. Augustine's
church-yard, she having expired at the house of her mother in Back-street ; the religious
ceremony being performed over her remains, her husband and children took their earthly
farewell, and her remains were left to moulder in its parent earth, But there is a certain description of people about, called " Resurrection Men," who make their trade to
dis-inter the dead bodies of such people as may be deemed good subjects for anatomizing,
and this poor woman's remains seems to have attracted the attention of these gentlemen,
and on Sunday night they proceeded to the church-yard, took up the body, and succeeded
in taking it to a house in College-street, for the purpose of dissection, which coming to
the husband's ears he immediately went to the house, but could not obtain admission for
some time, nor until he ascended up to a window, by the assistance of his friends, through
which he entered, and there discovered the mangled remains of the late partner of his
toils, they actually commenced their operations, having made incisions from the elbow to
the wrist of the left arm, it is also stated that her legs were cut, and her back broken, for
the purpose of putting the body in a bag ; the poor man seized the body, and it was interred a second time, but again taken up and recovered by the husband and interred a
third time. A stone bottle, containing spirits, was left in the grave.

Shepherd, Printer, No. 6, Broad Weir, Bristol.

Bodysnatching notices and newspaper cuttings

A receipt for three guineas for articulating the skeleton (attaching the bones together) was given to Dr Smith by J S Cock, dated December 13th, but no year was given; it may have been 1828, the same year the skin was used to bind the book. The book bound in Horwood's skin and his skeleton were in Smith's private museum at his house until his death. Smith had so many skulls at his house that he had them engraved with their names to identify who they were.

# CHAPTER SEVEN

## *Pillars of society*

Three generations of the Smith family with the Christian name Richard served the inhabitants of Bristol, the first a brewer, his son and grandson doctors. It was the youngest who was involved in the John Horwood case.

The first Richard Smith arrived in Bristol from Warminster in the early part of the eighteenth century and set up business as a brewer and maltster. He married Elizabeth Bradford, a shrewd and energetic woman. He was a man of elegance, with refined manners, fond of reading books and unfitted to his brewery business, which was principally managed by his wife. It was said at the time that no two people could be so unlike each other, he being slow in speech, mild and placid, while she was quick and irritable and knew how to scold. They were not a well-matched couple and a joke of the neighbours at the time was that Smith and his wife seemed to agree only in the getting of children, as eleven were born to them. They lived in a stone-fronted house in Counterslip, opposite the Baptist Church. Smith was Tory in politics and very well respected in the city. When he died in 1777 the brewing business continued in the hands of two of his daughters, Elizabeth and Ann.

The second Richard Smith was born on the 14th June 1748 in the house at Counterslip and at the age of nine was sent to be educated at Bristol Grammar School and later to Warminster Grammar School. At Warminster the discipline appears to have been too severe for his taste, causing him to abscond, taking with him a small bundle of clothes. Several days later he was found working with masons who were building a house. His parents were not very pleased and Winchester College, known for strict discipline, was selected to further his education.

Smith was flogged quite regularly for being idle, unmanageable, high-spirited and mischievous. With his school friends he was a regular at the local alehouse, where they would drink a toast to the 'Pretender', fights with locals were a regular occurrence, and he often robbed orchards and farmyards. This Richard Smith was clearly a conspicuous figure who caused trouble and annoyance in the everyday lives of the locals.

In 1762 he left college and returned home to fulfil his father's ambition for him to become a doctor. He was indentured to Dr John Townsend, surgeon at Bristol Infirmary, who also practised in Broad Street. Richard was just fourteen at this time and certain conditions as to his behaviour and conduct were written into his indentures; 'Taverns he shall not frequent; Dice he shall not play; Matrimony he shall not contract into' and so on. Townsend had a hard time trying to keep his apprentice in order. He did his best, but had many difficulties with him.

Richard went to London and did a course on midwifery at the Borough Hospital. On one occasion he was stopped by a senior surgeon while on his way to a birth dressed in a scarlet cloak and armed with a sword. It was pointed out to him that he looked dressed to take someone out of this world rather than bring someone into it.

When he returned to Bristol in 1768 he setup his own practice in his father's house in Counterslip, and in the same year he was appointed surgeon at St Peter's Hospital. He was married in 1771 to Augusta Calcott, the daughter of The Rev Alexander Calcott, master of the Free Bristol Grammar School. Their home was the last house in Charlotte Street on the corner with Queen's Square.

Although his practice was fairly successful, an accidental circumstance brought him rapidly to fame. The owner of a large brewery in Redcliffe Street dislocated his shoulder and a Dr Townsend was sent for. With the help of a number of workmen he tried to get the shoulder back in place, but everything he tried failed. He had just informed his patient that he was afraid he could not get the bone back in place when the brewer saw Smith riding past, and with the consent of Dr Townsend, he called him in. The shoulder muscles had been exhausted by the severe pulling they had received from Townsend, but Smith had barely begun to examine the shoulder when it popped back in, to the delight of the brewer and his workmen.

Smith's reputation as a doctor was made – even more so when in 1777 he was fortunate enough to restore life to a supposed drowned boy, for which he received the Royal Humane Society Medal.

In the December of 1785 he took up residence in College Green, opposite St Augustine's Church. He was tall, handsome, of slight but athletic build, with bright eyes and shining white teeth. He was kind-hearted, generous and fond of music and literature. He was described as an excellent companion, not easily angered but quick to resent minor troubles such as a bad hand at cards. He was impetuous and always ready to fight when the occasion arose. He was a good boxer and frequently took off his coat to anyone he saw ill-treating an animal.

In 1778 three candidates stood for election as Member of

Parliament for Bristol. Smith, a staunch Tory, got himself involved with writing anonymous letters under the name of 'Subscriber' to the newspapers and receiving opposing replies to his correspondence from 'Defector.' Day after day letters appeared from these two, full of recrimination and sarcasm aimed directly at each other. 'Defector' sent over forty letters filled with taunts about 'Roaring Catches', obviously meaning that 'Subscriber' was very fond of spending his evenings singing at the 'Catch Club.' Everyone soon became aware that 'Defector' was the quarrelsome Dr Rigge and 'Subscriber' was Smith.

Smith challenged Rigge to fight a duel to settle the matter, and he accepted. At dawn the next morning the parties met at the prearranged spot behind Brandon Hill. Both parties had their pistols loaded and were ready to fire when their seconds appealed to them to settle their differences in another way, otherwise there would be serious consequences. They pointed out that both of them had wives and children. Rigge was inflexible by nature, but being considered the aggressor in this instance he consented to make an apology, which Smith accepted.

Towards the end of May 1791, an unusually hot month, Dr Smith returned from a long ride in an exhausted state and very soon a sudden fever came on. After a partial recovery he relapsed, and he died on the 21st June, aged just 42. He left two children, Henry, who became an attorney, and Richard.

The third Richard Smith was born on the 28th June 1772 at his parents' house in Queen's Square, Bristol. The young Richard was educated at Bristol Grammar School and then studied medicine under his father until his father's death. He was then apprenticed to Godfrey Lowe, the senior surgeon at the infirmary. In 1796 Dr Joseph Metford resigned and he was appointed to the infirmary in his place.

Smith was married on 26th May 1802 at the church of St. Augustine the Less to Anna Eugenia Creswick. They set up home at 38 Park Road in a fashionable part of the city. From home he ran his private medical practice and set aside a room to exhibit his ever-increasing museum collection. His father had begun an anatomical museum and he continued expanding his father's hobby.

Many weird objects were collected over the years including his own milk teeth, as well as John Horwood's skeleton and the book bound in his skin. There were glass jars filled with preservatives containing all kinds of human body parts and curiosities. He continued to collect the rare and bizarre until his death, when the contents of his museum, under the terms of his will, was bequeathed to the Bristol Infirmary. At every opportunity when visitors arrived at his house he wasted no time in introducing them to his exhibits. Early in his career he showed great medical knowledge and ability as a speaker.

In 1802 two females, Maria Davies and Charlotte Bobbitt, abandoned a child and left it to die on Brandon Hill. They were tracked down, convicted of infanticide and subsequently executed on the gallows on St Michael's Hill. After execution their bodies were handed over to surgeons for dissection at the Bristol Infirmary, and the Mayor and Aldermen asked Smith to dissect the brain of one of the convicts. Smith of course took great pleasure in carrying out their request, giving a public lecture on the workings of the brain. His skill and dedication as a leading doctor and surgeon were rewarded in 1812, when he was promoted to the position of Senior Surgeon at Bristol Infirmary.

In 1814, two years after this promotion, a vault was excavated by workmen during repairs to St. Mary Le Port Church, and a lead coffin was discovered inside. Local historians convinced themselves that it was the resting place of Robert Yeomans a leading local Royalist executed in the city during the Civil War in 1643. On hearing this, Smith got himself involved in the opening of the lead coffin. The body was wonderfully preserved and Smith wasted no time in dissecting it and keeping the heart as an exhibit in his museum. Later it was proved that the body was not that of Yeomans.

Like his father Smith was a convivial, cheerful man, with a ruddy face and strident laugh, always laughing at his own stories. His social habits and excellent qualifications as a host were well known. In company of friends he was full of jollity and liked nothing better than singing songs and telling stories. He was a Freemason, introduced into the Royal Sussex Lodge in 1817 by his brother. He became Worshipful Master of that lodge in 1820 and Deputy Provincial Grand Master in 1830.

The Bristol Charities had the pleasure of his services and he became a Trustee in 1838. He also served on the Bristol Town Council from 1835. In 1841 a subscription was made to have his portrait painted by the artist J Branwhite, and this still hangs in the lodge room at the Infirmary. In his later years he was often seen in the city driving a gig, wrapped in a rough camlet coat with his white dog running underneath.

Richard Smith continued as the Senior Surgeon at Bristol Royal Infirmary until 24th January 1843, when he collapsed at the Philosophical and Literary Institution and died, aged 71 years. On the day of his funeral thousands lined the streets to pay their last respects. Shops and businesses closed for the day with their shutters drawn as a mark of respect. As the procession entered Temple Street, large numbers blocked its passage and they had to reform before entry could be gained to the churchyard at the Temple Church. After the service he was interred in a grave in the north west corner. The people of Bristol gave a respectful farewell to a devoted son of the city.

Smith had no direct blood heir and his last Will and Testament, dated 4th May 1840, provided for two of his brother Henry's children, Augusta Anne Smith and Elizabeth Creedy Smith, with one thousand pounds each. Henry's widow also received an income for life. The contents of his museum were bequeathed to Bristol Royal Infirmary, while everything else went to his wife. At his death he owned a property in Lower College Street, a public house named the Castle in Temple Street, an eating house in the Market Place, sixteen shares in the Bristol Union Insurance Company and a plot of land in Buckinghamshire. In Bath he owned a 'messuage' (house and curtilage) and shop and an interest in a property in Cheap Street.

His house at 38 Park Road was auctioned three days after his death. His wife was not present at this house in 1841, nor listed among the mourners at his funeral. Whether they were living as man and wife is unknown, but she had a house in Clifton and died there in 1864 aged 86 years.

# CHAPTER EIGHT

◦◦◦

## *The body trade*

Dr Richard Smith had a long career in his chosen profession. Surgery in those days was an extremely risky affair and the level of hygiene was very poor. Surgeons operated in unhygienic theatres, using crude instruments that were rarely cleaned between operations. Hands were not washed before or between surgeries and surgeons wore their everyday clothes for theatre duties.

Surgery at this time was defined as external diseases which required manual interference, including operations to reduce fractures, dislocations, the dressing of wounds and ulcers, removal of teeth, the opening of abscesses and all eye and skin diseases, and the surgeon had a monopoly on the treatment of venereal disease.

Lack of anaesthesia was also a problem. Surgery had to be performed very quickly and the only operations possible were amputations and the removal of growths or problems close to the body surface. The removal of fingers and toes was performed by placing the part to be removed on to a block of wood, positioning the chisel and striking it with a hammer. Patients had to be immobilized and kept as still as possible by assistants holding them down while the surgeon performed his task as fast as he could. Many died during the surgery from shock or pain, and if they survived on the table they were likely to die from blood loss or infection later.

Hospitals were not clean or efficient places of care and recovery. Bristol Infirmary was a charitable institution, where surgeons gave their services free and nursing was considered a lowly occupation with very poor pay and did not attract the dedicated people we know today. Twenty or so years after the death of Richard Smith, Florence Nightingale described the type of women employed in nursing as too weak, too drunk, too stupid and too bad to do anything else.

A problem for student doctors arose out of the difficulty of procuring bodies for dissection. Only the bodies of convicted murderers could legally be dissected under British law, and at this time only about 55 of these were available per year nationwide. People who died in hospitals ran the risk of their bodies being interfered with by the doctors. In general those wealthy enough to pay avoided the hospitals at all costs, preferring to be treated in their own homes. The poor had no choice but to take a chance on seeking treatment at the infirmary. The vulnerable and poor were used to experiment with new medication and treatments. Anything that worked was passed on to those who could afford to pay; the many failures were at the expense of the poor, who suffered the consequences.

The shortage of legal bodies for dissection led to the very profitable trade of body-snatching. Stealing a body was only a misdemeanour at Common Law, not a felony, and was punishable only with a fine or at worst imprisonment, rather than transportation or execution. The trade was in general lucrative enough for offenders to run the risk of detection, particularly as the authorities considered it a necessary evil. A relatively fresh corpse was worth around six pounds, and the Resurrection Men were tempted as it would take many weeks of hard graft to earn that amount by their own labour.

Richard Smith was learning his trade towards the end of the 18th century, a time of a population increase that resulted in the need for more doctors. The established medical men made it known that only by dissection could students be taught about the structure of the human body.

There is evidence of bodies being brought from London to Bristol by carriage disguised as luggage, at a cost of six guineas each. This would have been in the early days, before the Bristol surgeons devised their own plan to obtain them locally, in most cases free of cost. Three bodies at a time could be used in one session in student instruction. In all cases it was customary for the surgeon to make the first cut into the chest in the shape of a cross, indicating he was acting in God's name. By the time the first Dr Smith was practising surgery the use of illegal bodies was commonplace, and by the time his son was practising, it would have been in the surgeons' view their right, whether legal or not.

In Bristol there was alarm in the minds of the poor that their loved ones might be dissected, as a rumour had broken out that the surgeons were doing a little practical anatomy in the dead house at the infirmary. The infirmary authorities had difficulty managing these affairs. The result was that the key to the dead house was always in the keep of the Apothecary.

In 1806 a letter of complaint was received at the infirmary stating that those who died there were frequently found mutilated, nurses having been bribed to leave the coffins unclosed. They also claimed a corpse had been removed from the infirmary burial ground and found in the Coaching House at Dr Smith's residence in Park Row.

In later life Smith freely admitted his involvement in body-snatching, particularly about the time when he had been under instruction from the surgeon Frances Cheyne Bowles. 'We played the part of the Resurrection Men and procured subjects in turns' he said. 'In doing this we got ourselves into awkward scrapes at times. One night I escaped being shot by some soldiers occupying a burial ground in Johnny Ball Lane, but after being discovered I managed to make my escape unscathed. We frequently substituted old sacks filled with rubbish or sand in the dead house for a corpse, we did this undetected for many years. We had our own keys made for the dead house and went equipped with turnscrews, hammers, wrenching irons, nails and everything else we would likely need. The nurses and undertakers were allowed to go through the procedure of laying out the corpse and making the coffin secure. We then removed the corpse and substituted about the same weight with rubbish or sand, leaving the coffins secure as though never touched.'

Another incident involving Richard Smith concerns a medical student, John Danvers, who needed a brain to dissect. With the help of Smith he removed the head of a negro from a coffin in the dead house. They wrapped it in a large handkerchief, but as they walked towards their lodging in the dead of night, it fell from under Danvers' arm. It was a pitch black night and they were unable to locate it. Fearful of using a light in case of discovery by the watch they decided to leave it, thinking no one would know where it had come from.

After a brandy at their lodgings it suddenly occurred to them that enquiry would be made at the infirmary and they would be discovered. They returned to the spot at the end of the High Street, linked arms, walking in a straight line backwards and forwards for more than an hour until Danvers' foot struck the head. They retrieved it a considerable distance from where it was lost, as it had apparently rolled down the hill.

A number of instances made the press. In November 1812 a

child had been buried in Bedminster Churchyard. The following June the child's aunt had passed away, and on opening the grave the child's coffin was found empty.

In 1819 a reward was posted offering a fifty-guinea reward for the arrest of body-snatchers in the City of Bristol. A grave in St Augustine's burial ground had been robbed and the body of a female interred the preceding morning had been dug up and stolen by some person unknown. The notice informed the public that fifty guineas would be paid to any person giving information leading to the conviction of the offenders.

It transpired on the night in question that a man had been seen with a sack on his back entering the door leading to the upper floors of premises in Lower College Street. The woman who kept the greengrocer's on the ground floor informed neighbours, and the news quickly spread. A crowd gathered among them, including by chance a man who had buried his wife at St Augustine's the previous morning. He hurried back to the churchyard to discover the grave empty. Returning to the shop and unable to gain entry through the locked door, he got a ladder, entered the premises through the window and discovered his wife's body. Those involved fled, narrowly escaping the furious crowd with their lives.

Early on the 2nd November 1822 eight men, including several doctors, entered the graveyard at Brislington, Bristol and began their nefarious work of plundering a grave. A woman who had died at the infirmary had been laid to rest in the graveyard, and the grave robbers had nearly completed their task of 'resurrecting' her when Mr Yates of the nearby Lamb Inn had suspicions that something was amiss. Along with several constables he entered the graveyard and apprehended the grave robbers. A desperate battle was joined with the body-snatchers. Rapiers were snapped and pistols drawn, resulting in bloody noses and some broken heads among the doctors, one of whom received a severe wound to the face. Eventually the constables secured five of the men, the other three escaping.

The prisoners were locked up in the Lamb Inn until the following morning. A prosecution was brought against them and Mr Yates was charged with violent assault on one of the body-snatchers, who had received such a violent blow from Yates, who had hit him in the face with his pistol, that it had nearly taken off his nose. Mr Ward, the son of the sexton at the church, was later apprehended as an accomplice; he was a votary at the Church of St Crispin.

Yet when the men stood trial they were sentenced by the magistrates to be bound over as to their future conduct. A blind eye was turned to the serious charges of assault.

Dissection and grave robbing were taking place on an unbelievable scale, and without doubt the Smiths were responsible for this ghoulish culture. Many of the Bristol students became surgeons in the army, navy, military, as ships' doctors or in the colonies. The Bristol doctors defended their actions when an incident became public knowledge by saying dissection was necessary to further the education of their students. A letter printed in a local paper pointed out: 'if dissection is absolutely necessary for the good of society and does not hurt the bodies after death, the surgeons, their fathers, mothers, widows, wives, sons and daughters should give up their bodies for dissection.'

Grave robbing was finally brought to an end in 1832 by the Anatomy Act, which gave doctors the legal right to the bodies of the poor and unclaimed who died in workhouses.

The series of events that followed Eliza Balsom's fatal injury are well documented. She was struck by the stone on the 22nd January and the injury treated at home. On the night she was struck her brother cut her hair with scissors before shaving round the wound with his razor. At the suggestion of her friend Ann Fry, salt butter was put on the wound and covered with brown paper, while her mother's remedy was to treat the wound with ointment and bread poultice.

Eight days after the injury Eliza sought treatment at the infirmary. After having the wound dressed she was told to return the next day to have the dressing changed. When she returned the next day, 31st January, Dr Smith saw her in the waiting room and enquired what had happened to her. Eliza would have informed him how she got the injury, and it was then that he claimed her as his patient. During his consultation he informed her that she needed to be admitted, but Eliza was very reluctant, considering herself well enough to continue as an out-patient. She had since the injury continued in her normal household duties and had even been well enough to carry water from Jefferies Well and walk unaided the ten-mile round trip from her home in Hanham to the infirmary at Bristol. Smith would have none of it and insisted she be admitted to the ward under his care, and with great reluctance she eventually agreed.

On admission to the infirmary the poor lost ownership of their bodies to the surgeons, who then decided what was best for the patient in life or death. She was ten days under Smith's care on the ward before her health began to decline, becoming feverish and restless with a headache and the wound inflamed. Almost immediately he decided to perform a trephine operation on her skull, after consulting with his fellow surgeons.

Trephine surgery is the oldest operation known. It consists of drilling a hole into the skull up to 5 cm in diameter. Skulls with signs of trepanning have been found in every corner of the world, and it seems to have been fashionable on and off throughout history. It was practised in the Stone Age, in Ancient Egypt, in Greek and Roman pre-historic times, in the Far East and Middle East, China, Brazil, in the South Seas and Africa. Experts in these matters consider it was used at different times by different cultures for variety of reasons, including the practice of magic, religion, to bring luck, for sacrifice or to liberate bad spirits and demons. In the 18th and 19th centuries in the western world, doctors revived the practice for medical conditions such as severe headaches, fractures of the skull and head wounds. Not all surgeons agreed it had any benefit to the patient, and most thought the practice so dangerous that 'the surgeon himself must have fallen on his head.' Sir Astley Cooper wrote in 1839 'if you were to trephine you ought to be trephined in turn.'

The survival rate was practically zero at the time Smith trephined Eliza, and those undergoing this procedure usually died from haemorrhage or infection within days. The operation took up to sixty minutes. In Eliza's case the hole drilled in her skull was the size of a shilling. She died from infection.

After the inquest carried out by Smith, the body of Eliza was released by the Coroner to her family for burial. Not all her body, however – Smith kept her skull, which was in his pocket at Horwood's trial and then became one of his exhibits in his morbid private museum. This raises the question - did the family get Eliza's body or just a coffin filled with sand, like so many other Bristol citizens?

Smith had known of John Horwood's involvement in the assault since he had first met Eliza on the 31st January, but he did nothing to get him arrested until her death was certain. If she had beaten all the odds and a miracle had occurred, Smith's credibility as a surgeon would have greatly increased and we would probably never have heard of John Horwood.

It was claimed in some quarters that Smith had pursued John Horwood out of pity, sorrow and a desire for justice for Eliza. Could he have had a less noble motive?

By the time of Eliza's death in 1821 Smith was at the pinnacle of his career, a leading citizen of the City of Bristol. He socialized with the highest orders and enjoyed the best connections within the secrecy of the Freemasons and its brethren, behind their closed doors. Would such a man feel pity or sorrow for a poor country girl like Eliza and put himself to so much inconvenience and trouble in the name of justice?

In all his years as a surgeon Smith had never had a 'legal' body to dissect in public. Did the death of Eliza and her accusations against Horwood bring him such an opportunity, one which he seized with open arms?

One wonders if Smith carried out the trephination on Eliza in the full knowledge that she would be unlikely to survive it, and that on her death he could expect to secure at least part of her body for his own ends. Did he also think ahead to the possibility that her murderer's body would then become his property as well?

Smith certainly put himself to a lot of trouble and inconvenience. He sent for the magistrates to hear Eliza's deposition, had Horwood arrested and was a witness for the prosecution at his trial. Did he pursue John Horwood for his body? There is enough evidence to consider it a great deal more probable than sorrow, pity and justice. Smith was a surgeon, not a lawyer, and would benefit from a guilty verdict against John Horwood.

The Smith family had already had personal experience with a murder charge. Richard's brother Henry was a lawyer who practised in Bristol. In 1809 he faced a murder charge after killing his opponent in a duel. Rather than face the charge, he fled, heading north to Scotland then sailing to Portugal to join the Duke of Wellington's army. While a freeman he prepared his defence, later returning to Bristol to face the murder charge. He stood trial and was acquitted on a technicality. Henry was the ideal person to discreetly advise his brother at every stage of the case.

The British Medical Journal of November 1869 stated that doctors had examined the skull of Eliza and found no evidence of the abscess on the outer table which Smith had sworn on oath was the cause of her death. They had however found evidence of an abscess on the inner table, where he had operated.

Whatever his motives, we now know that it was not John Horwood who killed Eliza Balsom but the surgeon - Richard Smith.

# CHAPTER NINE

## *A decent burial*

After seeing the undignified and inappropriate way the remains were being stored at the University, we decided that we had to take action. We wondered if the new Bristol Museum of Life might be interested in displaying it with a narration of the story; seemingly they had planned to display the Book of Skin there. We offered it to them, but they turned it down as unsuitable. When we discovered the heartbreaking correspondence between the solicitors acting for John's family and Dr. Smith, who refused even to hand over to them what was left of the body after dissection to enable them to give him a Christian burial, we were glad the museum had turned down our offer.

Mary wrote to the University in the February 2010 asking for the release of the skeleton. They acknowledged the letter and informed us that the request had been passed to the legal department. Nothing was heard from them again until June 2010, when a letter informed us that the request was still being dealt with. On the 19th July a letter arrived confirming their conditions for the release of the skeleton. It stated:

'By virtue of this letter the University of Bristol agrees to give the skeleton of John Horwood to Mrs Mary Halliwell. Collection should be made by appointment with Angela Wells and at the expense of the collector. The skeleton is currently hung in a wooden case and this can be included in the collection. The University will have no further responsibility for the skeleton.'

After a family discussion, we decided that as the University had made use of the skeleton over so many years in teaching medical students, and the family had been denied release of the remains at the time of the execution, that they should be asked to contribute towards the funeral expenses. I informed them of our request.

On the 2nd September we received a letter from the Acting Chief Executive offering a 'minimalist cremation'. Any kind of cremation was completely out of the question, and the offer was declined. Another letter dated 29th September informed us that a funeral was too expensive and their first offer was as far as they would go.

Enquiries were made and we discovered that what they meant by 'minimalist cremation' was burning the remains in the way hospitals dispose of human waste. In disgust, we ceased all correspondence with the University.

Another consideration was - would a church allow a convicted murderer a Christian burial service and interment in their graveyard? John had had a grandmother, mother, two sisters and a brother buried at St Mary's Bitton. This church is where Eliza was interred, so we did not think it an appropriate place to lay him to rest. His father Thomas, brother Joseph and a sister are buried at Christ Church Hanham, so I contacted the vicar, the Rev. Pat Willis, who had no objection to John being interred there. However she was about to retire, so she instructed the Churchwarden, Mr Andy Bailey, to deal with it.

We now needed to locate one of the family graves, so we sent Mr Bailey the details: father, Thomas Horwood, 12th March 1845, brother Joseph Horwood, 14th October 1863, sister Mary Wiltshire, 15th January 1846. He replied that it was imperative to locate one of these graves as there was no room left in the burial ground.

Mary looked up a local undertaker in Hanham, E C Alderwick & Son, and wrote to them asking if they could give an estimate of cost to transport the skeleton from the University in Bristol to their funeral home in Hanham and arrange a basic funeral at Christ Church. We explained the story of John's execution and the refusal of the authorities to help with the cost. John had stood five feet six inches tall, but if his skeleton were dismantled a coffin only a little larger than his largest bone, the thigh bone, would be needed. We thought this might help in finding a burial plot if his relatives' graves could not be found.

A phone call was received from the funeral director, Austin Williams. We had a long conversation about the story of John Horwood and my aim to carry out his parents' wishes nearly two centuries after his death. He explained that John's story was of great interest to him personally and to his company, as well as to the community in general.

Later I received the following email: 'I can confirm that as a company we will be pleased to help you with the funeral and will cover many of the expenses that will be incurred. I would like to suggest that the skeleton of Mr Horwood remain in a complete state and we will supply a suitable coffin for the interment. With the families' blessing we would like to suggest that the funeral represents one which would have taken place at the time of his death, with the possibility of using a horse-drawn hearse.'

The undertakers arranged the release of the skeleton, and on the 12th October it was removed from the cupboard under the stairs at the University and taken to the funeral home in

Southville, Bristol. Meanwhile the Churchwarden, with the help of Austin, located the graves of John's father Thomas and the family grave of his brother Joseph. Austin then sought the permission of the Bishop to open the grave of Thomas to reunite his son with him.

In early November a meeting was arranged with the undertakers in Bristol, and we traveled down on the Sunday for a three-night stay. We settled on a date of 13th April and a time of 1.30, so that he would be interred exactly one hundred and ninety years to the minute, he had died on the scaffold.

By now the Bristol Press where beginning to show an interest. On the Monday BBC Radio Bristol broadcast a live interview with Austin and Mary. After that experience she found herself in front of a TV camera recording an interview with BBC Points West, and later that afternoon we gave an interview to the Bristol Evening Post. It was possibly the most traumatic Monday in her life.

On the Tuesday we visited Kingswood Museum to offer them the case John's skeleton had been kept in and the rope which had hanged him. This they gratefully accepted, telling us they would use it in a display about him that was already in progress. Meeting the residents of Kingswood revealed that they had a true feeling of sympathy for John and agreed that he had been unjustly treated all those years ago, which fully supported my effort to give him a Christian burial.

On returning home, within half an hour the phone rang – Mary was being asked to do a live interview on BBC Radio 5 that evening. The following day she appeared live on BBC TV Look North, the next morning Greater Manchester Radio and then we were interviewed by the *Wigan & Leigh Reporter*, our local newspaper.

The Bishop's Office confirmed that John would be permitted

burial in the grave of his father. As there was no resident vicar at Christ Church, Canon David Adams was appointed to take charge of the service.

John was arrested at his home in Grouty's Lane (now Furber Road) on the 15th February 1821, and he never saw Hanham again. It is ironic that the incident with Eliza took place at Jefferies Hill and his final resting place was to be in the churchyard of Christ Church, which is also on Jefferies Hill. At the time of the incident and for a long time before, this was the place were the rough colliers and equally rough stone quarry men met on their only day off work, Sunday. They staged bare knuckle fights, the champion of one clan fighting off the champion of another. It was here in 1798 that Jem Belcher became the boxing champion of England after defeating Bob Briton. Cock fighting and bull baiting also took place here.

The hill at that time was uncultivated land and was used as common ground for the grazing of donkeys, geese and pigs and as a playground for the local children. As you approach the church from Memorial Road, on your right is a road with the name Polly Barnes Hill, leading down a steep slope to Jefferies Hill Bottom. The spot where the brook runs at the bottom of the valley is probably the place were Eliza fell. John would have been higher up the hill, nearer to Church Road.

The foundation stone for the church was laid in February 1840 and consecrated in October 1842. Jefferies Hill had been used in the past for religious services and in the 1820s George Pocock, the grandfather of the famous cricketer W G Grace, had held a tent mission here for many years, periodically coming to preach himself. Services were held in the open air, in a tent or in a resident's cottage. It is also the place where the remembrance service was held for John the Sunday after his execution.

By early March arrangements for the funeral were complete. Research revealed that a poor person buried in 1821 would not have had the luxury of a horse-drawn vehicle; the coffin would have been carried by relatives or a wheeled funeral bier might have been used. The coffin would have been plain black with four metal rings to assist in lowering it into the grave. All of this information was taken into account by the funeral director in his arrangements.

The funeral was to be on the Wednesday 13th April 2011, leaving the funeral home at 12 noon to arrive at Christ Church at 12.30. Interment would be at 1.30, exactly 190 years to the instant after John had died on the scaffold.

The mourners began to arrive at the funeral home in High Street, Hanham at around 11 am. The skeleton of the deceased had been taken out of the case and laid out in a plain black coffin with four metal rings, two on each side. The coffin was lined with a soft white cotton material that stood out from the surrounding blackness of the wood of the coffin. Family members who chose to view the remains commented on the dignified way the skeleton had been laid to rest.

In the corridor adjoining the chapel of rest a very old funeral bier was waiting, its wooden frame and wheels polished and spotless waiting to do a task that it had not been asked to do for very many years. The coffin was closed and placed on the bier ready for John's last journey. A purple velvet drape was placed over the coffin and a tribute of flowers, including bluebells, cherry blossom and plain white blooms, was laid on top.

The four pall bearers took their positions two on either side, each holding a handle. A long-stemmed red rose was presented to each of the ten direct descendants who were in attendance, and they took their positions directly behind the bier, while the others followed behind. The procession proceeded at a slow walking pace, led by Austin Williams, the funeral director, on to the High Street. Traffic came to a halt on the busy thoroughfare. Rain had begun to fall and a number of umbrellas soon covered the heads of some of the mourners, but the downpour stopped as quickly as it started, although the dark clouds hung overhead threatening to strike again at any moment.

Onlookers appeared on the pavement, some taken by surprise, standing with heads bowed in mingled respect and amazement at the unusual funeral they were witnessing. The procession continued at a slow pace, turning off the main highway into Memorial Road and then making a right turn into Church Road.

A number of mourners stood at the church gates awaiting our arrival, together with newspaper reporters, photographers and TV crews. As we stopped at the church gate Canon Adams approached and greeted us.

After a short pause in the proceedings the coffin was raised from its resting place on the bier and placed on the pall bearer's shoulders. They followed the vicar as he began the short journey in prayer to the church entrance. Inside the mourners took their places to the soft tones of the music whispering from the organ. Canon Adams welcomed the congregation to what he called 'an opportunity to reflect on the life and death of a native of Hanham and a day of closure.' The first reading was Psalm 90 followed by the hymn *The Old Rugged Cross*.

Next there was a word of thanksgiving by Mary Halliwell, John Horwood's four-greats niece. She spoke to a congregation of around sixty, and began by thanking everyone who had supported the family by attending the service today, especially Austin Williams, the funeral director. She emphasised that without his kind generosity the funeral might not have taken place. Turning towards the coffin and touching it tenderly, she spoke directly to her ancestor: 'Well John, you have finally come home to Hanham, the place of your birth. We have brought you home to lie in rest with your father, Thomas. Rest in peace John, and may God bless you.'

Martin Loughran, who had been involved along with his mother Pat Constable in advising on the research, had travelled from Hove near Brighton to attend the service. He told the congregation:

'A great injustice was done to this young man and today there is a profound sense of spiritual and moral justice for a family who for nearly two hundred years have been denied the right to pay their respects to a loved one. His father Thomas fought hard to get his remains to give him a Christian burial and that was denied him. Was John guilty? He threw the stone that brought about a chain of events for which he was partly responsible, but was he culpable on his own? I think the majority of you would feel not. John was in the wrong place at the wrong time and he paid the ultimate price for what he did with his life.'

Martin read an 'Ode to John Horwood' which he had written for the occasion:

*Home to Hanham, John, 'twas the family's dearest will*
*Where once you stood tall upon Jeffries Hill*
*Put to death as a man yet merely a boy*
*Oh those bitter sweat tears are those of joy*
*The wrong place in history, fable nor myth*
*You were fated to die, at the hands of Smith*
*For the unrequited love of Eliza, you lost your life*
*As she declined your proposal, to become your wife*
*Today and forever you shall never once be alone*

*Why, oh why John Horwood, why that deadly stone?*
*A family's unconditional love & oceans of cascading tears*
*Have lived for this very day, one hundred & ninety years*
*There's a peaceful smile now upon every related face*
*For today you shall rest at home, in your rightful place*
*Pray for those who wronged you, today you're set free*
*Seated at God's table, as well you should be*
*Whether it be sunshine or rain upon your face*
*The Master's House, is now your resting place*
*Rest Dear John, Sleep Dear John, for we too must part*
*Forever in our thoughts, eternally in our heart*

Martin J Loughran MA
All Rights Reserved © Forever Thoughts MMX1

John Harwood, four-greats grand nephew, read a Bible reading from Romans 8, appropriate for this occasion as it had been read at the memorial service held on Jeffries Hill the Sunday following the execution in 1821.

This was followed by the song *You Raise Me Up*. Next was the address by Canon Adams, who surprised some of those present with his knowledge of the circumstances surrounding the life of John and his death. He concluded this part of the service with the Lords Prayer. The Hymn *How Great Thou Art* was sung next, and then he began the Commendation and Blessing.

The recessional hymn *Going Home* was sung solo by Josie (Harwood) Newell, another four-greats niece. A number of the congregation failed to follow the cortege out of the church to the grave, choosing instead to listen to the voice of Josie putting so much feeling into this appropriate and beautiful hymn.

After the mourners had slowly followed the coffin to the graveside, at precisely one thirty, John Horwood was lowered into the grave to be united with his father. As Canon Adams moved aside, each family member filed past in turn to make a final farewell, each giving up their red rose to the grave. The adjoining grave is occupied by John's sister Mary and a few yards away under a blossoming cherry tree lies another Horwood grave, that of John's brother Joseph and his family.

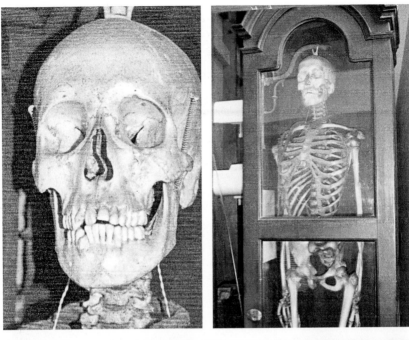

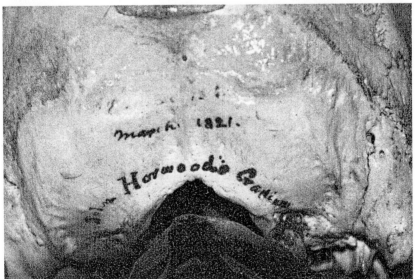

Horwood's skeleton and the engraving on the rear of his skull

John Horwood, convicted of the wilful murder of Eliza Balsom. The body delivered to Mr. Richard Smith of the City of Bristol, surgeon, to be dissected and anatomised on this 13th day of April 1821.

John Horwood, a boy of 18, had courted Eliza Balsom but she rejected his addresses and in a fit of anger he flung a stone at her from a distance of 40 yards and struck her on the head. This occurred on January 26th, 1821. She fell but was not stunned and walked home, where her friends applied ointments and a broad poultice. She was then well until January 31st, when she walked from Kingswood to the Infirmary. She did well at first but 'inflammatory symptoms' supervened. She was trephined by Richard Smith, who claimed to have found an abscess under the bones of the skull. She died on February 21st, 1821.

It is recorded that Horwood was brought before his victim in the Infirmary by a magistrate and because Horwood appeared to be indifferent, he was shown the case containing the skeletons of Davis and Gobbett. Horwood was tried before the Recorder, Sir Robert Gifford, and condemned to death.

The defence that the abscess on the brain might have been caused by the unclean dressings put on the wound was suggested in the Court but was not pursued. The skull of Eliza Balsom shows subperiosteal new bone on the inner table but no obvious signs of osteomyelitis associated with the indentation on the outer table. It seems possible that there was an extra-dural abscess associated with the trephining rather than the original injury.

Horwood was executed in public outside the New Jail, the gates of which still exist in The Cut near the General Hospital. The crush of spectators was so great that notices were put up warning people of the danger of being pushed into the water.

Despite the efforts of Horwood's friends and relatives his body was dissected by Richard Smith in front of an audience of 80 people. His skin was removed and tanned by Richard Smith, who had received instructions and materials for tanning from the Sheriffs of the City, both of whom were tanners. The skin was dressed and used to bind a book consisting of the case notes and account of the trial of Horwood, together with a phrenological chart. This book is still kept in the Board Room of the Bristol Royal Infirmary.

Richard Smith, Jun. was the son of a surgeon at the Bristol Royal Infirmary and was himself senior surgeon from 1812 to 1843. He was a great collector and the founder of the Bristol Royal Infirmary Museum. Before he is criticised for his part in the gruesome affair of Horwood it should be realised that he lived in a time when the "Bloody Code" of English law was at its height. It was only 10 years previously that the Archbishop of Canterbury with other bishops voted against a bill for abolishing capital punishment in cases of stealing goods of less value than five shillings.

Infirmary notice on side of skeleton case

Book of Human Skin, on display in the M Shed, Bristol

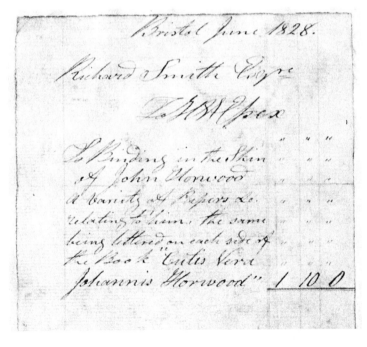

Bookbinder's bill for the Book of Human Skin

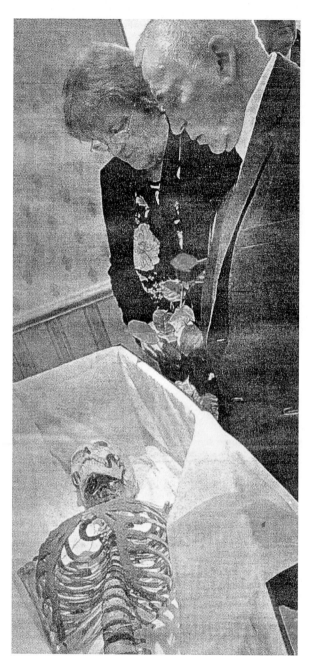

Mary and Dave
Halliwell with the
skeleton before
burial
(photo Bristol
Evening Post)

Funeral bier with pallbearers at the undertakers in Hanham

Relatives at the graveside

Arrival at Christ Church, Hanham

Journey to the grave

Interment

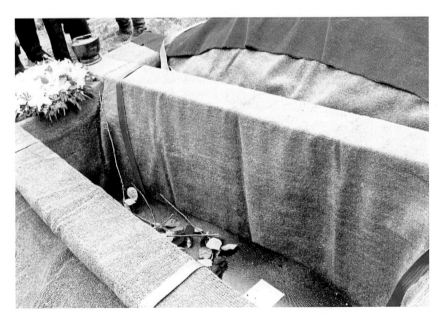

Coffin in grave

Funeral cortège (photo Daily Telegraph)

The funeral service (photo from the internet)

Mary Halliwell at John's graveside (photo Bristol Evening Post)

John Horwood's final resting place

(family photo)

# EPILOGUE

When I began my research into the maternal side of my family, I never expected to find a real skeleton under lock and key in a cupboard in Bristol. None of my existing family had ever heard of John Horwood or knew they had a convicted murderer in the family. Maybe the story was not passed from generation to generation, or had just been forgotten over the passage of time.

The result of nearly three years of research exposed a story of a young country boy and girl falling in love. Eliza chose to end the relationship and the immature John, unable to accept she no longer wanted him, set off a chain of events that cost them both their lives.

By throwing that stone John put Eliza into the hands of Dr Richard Smith, who first messed up her treatment, then encouraged her to make allegations against her attacker. Once the allegations were in the hands of the magistrates Smith personally took out the arrest warrant and had him arrested. He questioned him at Eliza's bedside, carried out the post mortem examination on Eliza's body and gave evidence as a prosecution witness at his trial. He categorically and without leaving any room for doubt gave the cause of death as an abscess on the outer table of the skull, and convinced the jury that the blow from the stone thrown by John Horwood had killed her. After the sentence he secured the murderer's body to dissect in public, an opportunity which he made full use of by showing off his skill as a surgeon - not as the sentence was intended, to educate the medical students, but to impress his friends and associates in the city. Even a place in the dead house was reserved for his own wife.

Once Smith had his claws into John Horwood, that poor youth stood no chance of justice. Smith wanted a legitimate body to dissect, and John became his victim - just like Eliza.

The British Medical Journal of October 1869, 26 years after Smith's death, clears John Horwood of the murder of Eliza Balsom. The surgeons who reviewed the case and examined Eliza's skull stated that the abscess was on the inner table of the skull and caused by the trephine operation conducted by Smith.

Eliza would have survived the wound inflicted by John Horwood. It was the surgeon's intervention, not the stone, that killed her.

John no longer hangs from a brass hook in a display case with a rope around his neck, as he had done for the past one hundred and ninety years.

He is now at rest with his father Thomas, and a memorial stone now marks the grave. The rope and case are now on public display at the Kingswood Museum, along with a narration briefly telling the story. The Horwood Papers (Book of Skin) is on display at the Bristol M Shed Museum.

The family can at last put closure on an unexpected discovery that has changed the direction of the Horwood family history.

Mary Halliwell

Dave Halliwell
Leigh, Lancashire
June 2012

# SOURCES & REFERENCES

John Horwood Papers, Dr. Richard Smith – Bristol Records Office, now on public view in the M Shed Museum, Bristol.

*History of Bristol Royal Infirmary, 1917*, G. Munro Smith MD

*A Short Narration of the Life & Death of John Horwood* - 1821 Philip Rose

*History of Kingswood Forest* - 1891, Baine

*Bristol Times & Mirror*

*Felix Farley's Bristol Journal*

Last Will & Testament of Richard Smith, proven 1843 - Public Record Office

*British Medical Journal*, 2nd October 1869

*Tanned Human Skin* - Lawrence S. Thompson

*Brain & Mind* Magazine 1997, Sabbatini

*The Neurologist*, Volume 5 Number 4, 1999

Baptism/Marriage/Death Records - Bristol & Avon Family History Sciety.

Hanham Christ Church Parish Magazine

Notes of Rev. Roberts, Methodist Minister - Marie Forse of Hanham